HOLLYWOOD

TRICKS OF THE TRADE

This book was devised and produced by Multimedia Publications (UK) Ltd

Editor: Richard Rosenfeld
Production: Karen Bromley
Design: John Strange and Associates
Picture Research: David Sutherland

Copyright © Multimedia Publications (UK) Ltd 1986

First published in the United States of America 1986 by Gallery Books, an imprint of W.H. Smith Publishers Inc., 112 Madison Avenue, New York, NY 10016

ISBN 0 8317 4240 2

Typeset by Falcon Graphic Art Limited
Origination by Brian Gregory Associates
Printed by Cayfosa, Barcelona, Spain

Dep. Leg. B - 11527-1986

Endpapers: Christopher Reeve wired up for flying in **Superman II** (1980).

Page 1: Roddy McDowall in Oscar-winning makeup for **Planet of the Apes** (1968).

Pages 2-3: A spectacular motorboat stunt by Jerry Comeaux in the James Bond movie **Live and Let Die** (1972).

Pages 4-5: Broiled ape on the menu in the supercolossal 1976 remake of **King Kong**.

HOLLYWOOD

TRICKS OF THE TRADE

Alan McKenzie   Derek Ware

GALLERY BOOKS
An Imprint of W. H. Smith Publishers Inc.
112 Madison Avenue
New York City 10016

CONTENTS

SPECIAL EFFECTS

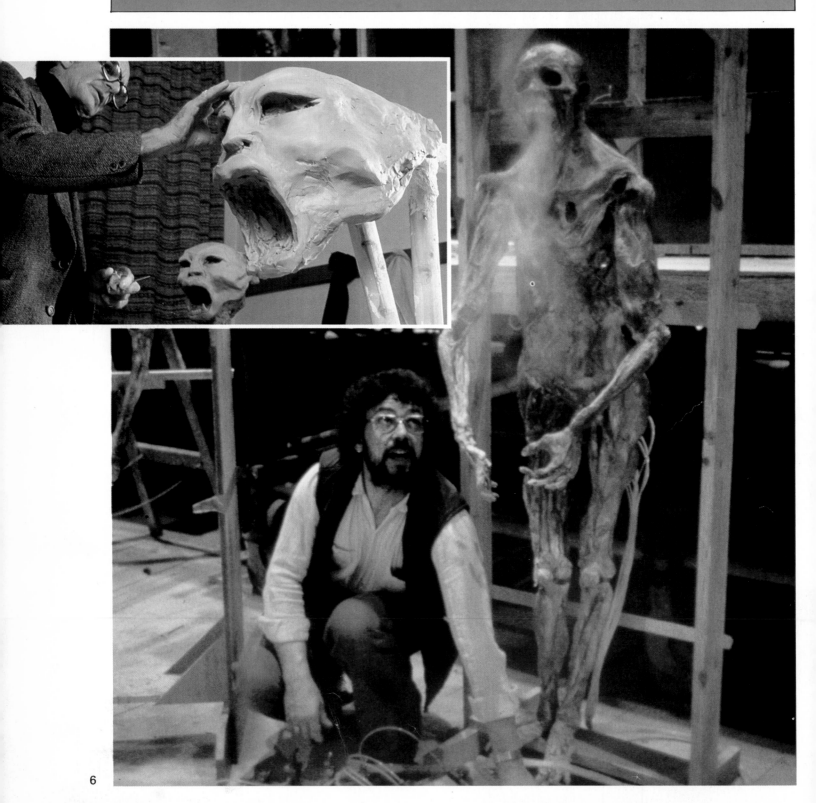

Main picture:
A technician plugs a dummy corpse into its control panel prior to filming the "Well of the Souls" scene in Steven Spielberg's **Raiders of the Lost Ark** (1981).

Inset:
A strange way to make a living . . . Models such as these require the skills of craftsmen whose work may extend months before and after principal photography.

"Special effects are like blind faith – you have to tell your man what you want to do and hope that when you get there he's figured out how to do it!"
Brian De Palma, director of **Carrie** (1976) and **The Fury** (1978).

There have always been special effects in the movies, but never so many and on such a scale as today. They are the new lifeblood of Hollywood, almost literally launching some of the biggest ever box-office hits into outer space, including **E.T. The Extra-Terrestrial** (1982), **Indiana Jones and the Temple of Doom** (1984), the **Star Wars** trilogy, **Close Encounters of the Third Kind** (1977), **Superman I** and **II** (1978 and 1980) and the immensely successful James Bond films of the early Sixties.

While movie fans worldwide revel in the sheer size of alien spaceships and the superhuman achievements of Superman and the like, few have any idea how such extraordinary effects are achieved. Broadly speaking, special effects break down into *visual effects* (or *trick photography*), where the illusion is created by "tampering" with the camera, and *mechanical effects*, achieved by "tampering" with the props. Equally important are *makeup* and *stunts*. Always remember, though, that while all these categories (with their many sub-divisions) are dealt with individually within this book, they are rarely used in isolation on the film set. In most movies, individual scenes will comprise of many of these techniques . . . in fact six or seven may even be required for just one shot!

Such effects are at their best not when the work of producer, technicians, stunt men and makeup artists gets in the way of the film, holding up the act of belief to ridicule, but when it easily merges with all the other vital components, from dialogue and pace, to acting and viewpoint, to ensure that the audience's disbelief is completely and magically suspended from the first frame of the first reel to the very end.

VISUAL EFFECTS

There's a marvelous joke in Mel Brooks' comedy Western movie **Blazing Saddles** (1974) when Gene Wilder as the Wako Kid reaches for his guns. No sooner do his hands move than the camera cuts to the dozen or so bad guys lined up against him. In that same instant, the first shot sounds and the first villain is disarmed. A withering hail of lead later and they are all helpless. On the sound of the last shot, the camera cuts back to Wilder, smugly sitting on his horse with his arms folded.

When described like this, the scene is unlikely to raise even a faint smile, for its comic potential can only be realized in visual terms. When filming the scene, the director relied on just three takes. In the first, Gene Wilder reached for his guns; in the second, the bad guys had their guns shot out of their hands; and the last is a shot of Wilder looking smug with arms folded. To achieve all this, the cameraman stopped the camera between each shot. Later, the editor cut the film together, compressing the time element to make Wilder seem impossibly fast on the draw.

This basic technique of trick photography was the first of its kind, apparently invented by the Frenchman Georges Méliès in 1896. When gathering footage for his gritty documentary about the Place de l'Opéra in Paris, he was busily cranking away at the passing traffic when his camera jammed and he was forced to stop for a minute or two to free the film. He then started cranking again without giving a thought to what the film would look like.

When Méliès developed and projected the film, he was amazed to see a weird transformation come over the street scene at the point where his camera had jammed. Men suddenly became women, a horse and carriage mysteriously turned into a tramcar. By complete accident the basic principle underlying *model animation* and *cel animation*, as well as editing, had been discovered – and the world of film was ready for a great leap forward.

Méliès quickly realized the commercial potential of his discovery. Very soon he was turning out hundreds of short "trick" films. The ideas were crude compared with today's post-**Star Wars** standards; for example, Méliès would simply point his camera at a chair and start turning the handle; a girl would walk into view and sit down; Méliès would stop cranking while the girl was replaced with a skeleton and then start again. Consequently, audiences were fooled into thinking that the girl had been turned into a bony apparition. 7

Cel animation

Motion pictures are produced by taking a rapid succession of still photographs – usually 24 frames per second (fps) – on a continuous strip of film. When this strip is run through a movie projector at the same speed, the image on the screen appears to move, via a trick of eyesight, called *persistence of vision*. This simply means that we are unable to see 24 pictures each second as a series of still pictures. Instead, we see them as *one* continuous moving picture. Now imagine if instead of 24 still photographs of real people passing through the projector every second, a film maker uses drawings. This is cel animation or cartoons.

The earliest films to use drawings rather than people were created by J. Stuart Blackton, who first used cartoon animation in his 1906 short film, **Humorous Phases of Funny Faces**. Although the Frenchman Emile Cohl produced a short film in 1908, using animated stick men for its characters, it took pioneering newspaper cartoonist Winsor McCay another three years to create the first "conventional" animated cartoon. His film of his own cartoon creation entitled **Little Nemo in Slumberland** made its debut in 1911.

McCay enjoyed a run of success as a cartoon animator, creating instant hits such as **Gertie the Dinosaur** and **The Sinking of the Lusitania**. But the major drawback with McCay's methods was that each drawing that went into a scene was drawn from scratch, including the backgrounds. This was immensely time-consuming and expensive, and if not done accurately made the images on the screen appear to wobble.

In 1914, however, cartoon animator Earl Hurd proposed that if the non-moving elements of an animated frame were drawn on paper, then the moving elements could be drawn on celluloid, or "cels", and laid over the top. In this way, only the moving elements would need to be drawn anew for each frame; the background needed to be drawn just once. Using this principle, cartoon animation began its long and well-documented career. Over the next forty years or so, cel animation made international stars out of Mickey Mouse, Bugs Bunny and a host of others.

In 1956 the MGM Studios asked Walt Disney Productions to provide such animated effects for their science fiction epic **Forbidden Planet**. The Disney team had already developed a whole array of animation tricks to enhance their first feature film **Snow White and the Seven Dwarfs** (1936). But for **Forbidden Planet** they wanted an even more dazzling range of effects, from a roaring, semi-invisible monster from the id and the colorful and majestic machinery of the Krell, to the retro-rockets of flying saucer C-57D. Although these effects are clearly recognizable as cartoon animation in the finished version, this doesn't detract from the film's success.

One of the most effective scenes takes place when the monster from the id attacks the saucer, while the ship's crew fight it off with laser guns. Hollywood production designer Joe Alves, who today designs movies for Steven Spielberg, was an assistant with Disney at the time and remembers how the id attack

8

scene was done. The sequence was created first by drawing the creature in crayon on animation paper which gave the impression that the creature was semi-invisible. The laser blast effects were added on separate cels. Then all the elements were superimposed over the live action film to complete a scene that until then had only shown the crew of the C-57D pointing guns that wouldn't fire at a monster that wasn't even there!

Startling as these special effects were, they didn't cause a sudden rash of imitations. In fact film makers avoided cel animation for years, probably because it looked too much like a special effect. Then, in 1963, Alfred Hitchcock dramatically reintroduced the technique in his masterpiece **The Birds**.

This is an extremely effective horror film in which the villain wasn't a monster in the traditional sense, but a part of nature gone haywire. But how did Hitchcock get the birds to "attack" the actors? Three techniques were used: first, a large proportion of the birds were actually small groups of live birds, photographed diving against plain backgrounds and later superimposed, often in several layers, over live-action footage; second, footage of live birds was used as *back projection* plates; and third, some of the birds were in fact animated models.

These days, cel animation is one of the least used special effects techniques. It turns up most often when lighting effects are needed, though it has found a new, if limited, lease of life providing the saber effects in the **Star Wars** movies. Cel animation is also the standard method for creating laser weapon effects, as in **Star Trek** (1979), when the spaceship *Enterprise* locks its phasers onto a Klingon target.

Model animation

The governing idea behind this technique is that a flexible model is photographed one frame at a time while an assistant moves the model in tiny increments between exposures. When the film is projected, it appears as though the model is moving autonomously.

The technique was created and pioneered by the film maker Willis O'Brien who, in the closing months of 1914, made a minute-long film about a caveman and a dinosaur. The film so impressed the Edison Company, one of the pioneering giants of the early cinema, that they hired him to make their animated dinosaur comedies.

O'Brien's earliest models were constructed out of modeling clay. But the enormous number of movements needed to put even a few minutes of action   9

onto film took its toll on the flimsy, flexible sculptures. Clearly a more sophisticated approach to the model-making side of the technique was needed. O'Brien solved the problem by using jointed wooden skeletons for his creatures. A body of clay was molded over the skeleton, and then a skin of fine canvas was stretched over the body. Finally, the model was painted before being put through its moves for the camera.

After a couple of years, the Edison company lost interest in O'Brien's stop-motion dinosaur films but in 1918 O'Brien teamed up with another dinosaur enthusiast, Herbert Dawley, to produce what is generally regarded as the first dramatic stop-motion movie, the five-minute **The Ghost of Slumber Mountain** (1919). Since Dawley attempted to claim all the credit for creating the animated creatures, the two men split up. Nevertheless, **The Ghost of Slumber Mountain** attracted such a lot of attention that O'Brien was contacted by Watterson Rothaker in the early Twenties to work on a feature-length adaptation of Sir Arthur Conan Doyle's **The Lost World** (1925).

At this stage, O'Brien's models were a good deal more complicated than the earlier wooden skeleton versions. With the aid of a young sculptor, Marcel Delgado, O'Brien created a horde of prehistoric monsters by sculpting foam rubber over elaborate metal skeletons. Some of the models even contained bladders which could be inflated with compressed air, so that the creatures appeared to breathe.

In 1922, while in the United States, Conan Doyle spoke to the annual gathering of the Society of American Magicians. After all the assembled conjurors had revealed their tricks, he outperformed them all. In a brief speech he explained that there was nothing supernatural in what the audience was about to see, and then projected a test reel of O'Brien's animation for **The Lost World**. The demonstration was so effective that it made the headlines in the *New York Times* the following day.

Herbert Dawley, O'Brien's earlier collaborator, read about the demonstration and promptly threatened to sue, though nothing came of the threat. All in all, the stunt had proved a spectacular success and work continued on the film until its release in 1925.

The Lost World was a big breakthrough in the history of movie special effects because it showed live actors in the *same* shots as the model dinosaurs. O'Brien used two different methods to achieve this effect. The simplest trick was to mask off the appropriate area of his frame while shooting the model footage, then double expose the actors in, performing

Above:
Perseus (Harry Hamlin) takes on two giant scorpions in **Clash of the Titans** (1981). The scorpions are miniature animated models set in front of a small back-projection screen, onto which is projected footage of Hamlin swinging his sword at imaginary opponents. The system works well enough but is, in fact, rather old-fashioned and inferior to the system used by Phil Tippett and his crew on **The Empire Strikes Back** (1980), which was made around the same time.

against a carefully matched background. The more complicated method was used for the scene in which a brontosaurus rampaged along a London street, as extras scattered in terror. For this part of the film the dinosaur was animated against a white background and the image was later combined with that of a street scene with the terrified extras. This was, in effect, the earliest form of *traveling matte* and was used extensively in special effects movies until a better process came along in 1932, just in time for **King Kong** (1933).

Since **The Lost World** O'Brien had been laboring in a dark corner of the RKO studio on a project of his own called **Creation**, which was later canceled by the new studio management. However, RKO's assistant studio head, Merian Cooper, felt that there was mileage to be squeezed from O'Brien's work and convinced RKO boss David Selznick to give the go ahead on another project, **King Kong**. More than fifty years later, **King Kong** is still one of the best remembered monster movies of all time, featuring Kong battling with dinosaurs and carrying in his giant hand the beautiful and screaming Fay Wray.

To achieve such effects, O'Brien did far more than just move his models about according to the script. He treated his models as *actors*, giving each its own convincing character. A good example occurred in Kong's battle with the tyrannosaurus when, having killed the fearsome creature by levering its jaws apart, Kong stands over the fallen reptile lifting its limp head off the ground and letting it fall back, as if finally checking that the monster is really dead.

In the wake of **King Kong**, O'Brien provided model animation for a range of other films including **Son of Kong** (1933), **Mighty Joe Young** (1949) and **The Black Scorpion** (1957). Film maker Ray Harryhausen has also built his career on his skill at model animation. Having worked with O'Brien on **Mighty Joe Young**, he branched out on his own and, after a stint making monster movies in the 1950s, found his niche with **The Seventh Voyage of Sinbad** (1958). More Sinbad films followed until, in 1981, he had a blockbuster hit

In this scene from **King Kong** (1933), everything you can see is a model. The figure of Kong is only 1½ feet tall and the man is about 6 inches tall. Both are fully jointed models, animated by Willis O'Brien.

12

Animator Stephen Archer, who assisted Ray Harryhausen on **Clash of the Titans** (1981), manipulates his crystal spider in **Krull** (1982). This effect was achieved by using the standard stop-motion animation process rather than the more sophisticated, computer-controlled animation of **The Empire Strikes Back** (1980) and **Dragonslayer** (1981).

with **Clash of the Titans**. Other successful exponents of stop motion are Jim Danforth, who was responsible for **Seven Faces of Dr Lao** (1964) and David Allen, who created the animation effects for **The Howling** (1981).

However, the big drawback with stop motion is that the images tend to look jerky, unlike film of living creatures which tends to be slightly blurred. So, while working on the animation of the two-legged Taun-Taun creatures seen on the planet of Hoth in **The Empire Strikes Back** (1980), model animator Phil Tippet decided to make the scene more convincing by introducing a blur into the footage. The effect was a great success though he was reluctant to explain exactly how he had done it. Later it was revealed that the effect had been achieved by using motors to move the model slightly at the precise moment when the frame of film was exposed. Such motors had first been introduced to model work for the spaceship scenes in **Star Wars** (1977); **The Empire Strikes Back** was the first use of the system for fully-jointed models. The system is called *motion control*.

The idea of using motion control to move articulated models was taken one step further with **Dragonslayer** (1981). For the scenes in which the dragon chases the hero Galen through a cave, the model was moved not by the animator's hands, but by rods connected at one end to the model's feet and at the other to a system of gears turned by stepping motors. There were three such motors attached to each of the dragon's four limbs, plus a further two sets to work the head and body, making a total of 18 motors, plus one to move the whole assembly backward or forward. The entire system was computer controlled and was so efficient that the dragon could have been photographed moving "live" if necessary.

Computer animation

As computers become increasingly smaller and sophisticated, so the boundaries of computer animation are being pushed back. In the Sixties it became possible to create "wire" drawings of an image, with all sides visible at once, and photographically accurate paintings of the most complicated shapes imaginable. The development of high-resolution laser etching devices has even enabled complex video images to be transferred to conventional film with much greater clarity than could be achieved using a movie camera.

Computer animation was used for some sequences of **Star Wars**, including the targeting computer read-   15

Charlton Heston and Monica Lewis above a city devastated by an **Earthquake** (1974) (*below right*). The destroyed city is an elaborate matte painting created by Albert Whitlock (*below*). Adding considerably to the illusion are the plumes of smoke which rise convincingly from the ruins. Whitlock achieved this effect by filming small columns of smoke in a large darkened soundstage, then superimposing this footage over his matte painting. This combined strip of film was matted together with the film of Heston clinging to the ruined skyscraper set.

outs used by the rebel pilots as they attacked the Death Star, and for the landing readouts seen in **Alien** (1979) as the spaceship *Nostromo*, with the doomed crew, touches down on the mysterious planet. The technique was taken to much greater extremes in the 1982 Walt Disney movie **Tron** which went about as far over the top with computer animation as **Forbidden Planet** had gone with cel animation. **Tron**'s effects were interesting, but it was difficult to see how these effects could ever be applied to a film where realism is required. Like cel animation, it seems that computer animation has a better future as an independent artform than as a tool of the special effects technician.

Glass painting

During the Silent era of Hollywood it was common practice for whole scenes to be shot against painted backdrops. The big step forward came in the early Twenties when Ralph Hammeras of Realart Pictures hit upon the idea of combining live-action footage with scenic paintings. For example, when painting a moonlit scene of an island, he decided to achieve greater realism by adding *real* water. He photographed the painted scene as far as the shore line, then added the footage of the water, illuminated by the sun's (not the moon's) rays. That was the beginning of a more sophisticated technique that later became known as the glass shot.

Up until this time the studios had had to build, for many films, street sets two, three and four stories high. Using this new idea, it now only became necessary to build a set one story high. The other stories of the building were painted, using opaque material, on

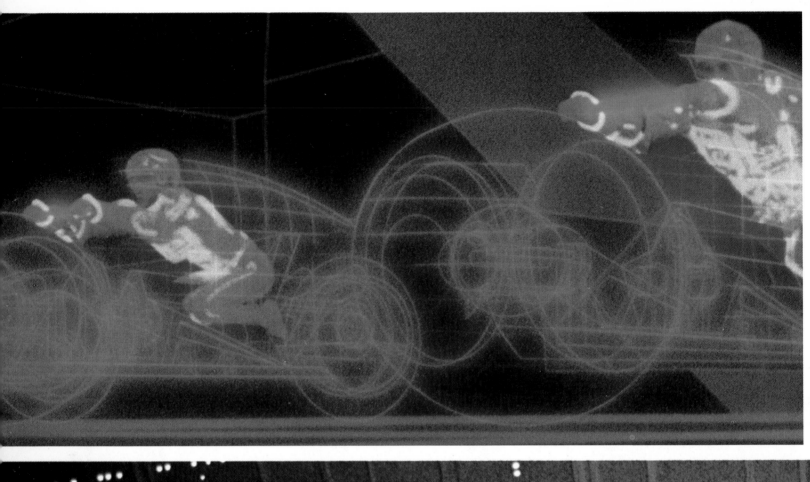

a plate of glass, five feet by six feet, and placed in front of the top half of the lens eight feet away.

The technique was so successful that in 1928 Hammeras was nominated for an Oscar for his work on Alexander Korda's **The Private Life of Helen of Troy** (1927), which made extensive use of his glass-painting method. Hammeras also contributed to O'Brien's version of **The Lost World**, and invented process photography, or back projection as it is better known.

So if when watching an old movie, made between 1927 and 1933, you see a set that rises much above the level of one story, the chances are that you will actually be looking at a glass painting! By 1933, though, glass painting was pushed aside by the arrival of matte painting or *stationary matte*.

Stationary matte

The stationary matte technique is a process by which a glass painting can be combined with live action footage, *after* the live footage has been filmed. These paintings are more properly called matte paintings to differentiate them from the older style glass paintings and were invented by glass painter Percy Day in the early Thirties. Day was asked to do a glass shot of a busy Paris boulevard but he found the task too difficult. To overcome this problem he used a technique from still photography whereby he would matte off areas of the frame. He put a mask in front of the camera to hide everything but the first floor of a

Left:
The computer-generated "light-cycles" form around their pilots in Walt Disney's computer-animation extravaganza **Tron** (1982). This was the first movie to use computer animation in place of regular cel animation. Sadly, the substitution doesn't work too well, as the computer-animated elements lack the dynamics of conventional animation. But then conventional animation has had 80 years' head start on the computer variety. . .

Below:
This scene features one of the better matte paintings seen in **The Empire Strikes Back** (1980). The only "real" elements of this scene are Darth Vader (played by Dave Prowse), the gallery on which he stands, Luke (Mark Hamill) and his perch. The background is a painting.

building and he added other sections later, of an architectural design more in keeping with the rest of the film. This simple process created the first matte shot. Shortly afterwards, the matte painting method replaced glass painting, and has become firmly established as the mainstay of the special effects team's repertoire. The original **King Kong** contained some remarkable matte paintings. Peter Ellenshaw provided some for **Things to Come** (1936), **The Thief of Bagdad** (1940) and more recently, **The Black Hole** (1980). His son, Harrison Ellenshaw, is also a matte painter and contributed paintings to **Star Wars** and **Tron**.

Other prominent matte artists include Albert Whitlock, who painted additional scenery for **Earthquake** (1974), **The Hindenburg** (1975) and several Hitchcock movies, and Matthew Yuricich, who created paintings for **Close Encounters of the Third Kind** and **Blade Runner** (1982).

There is no doubt that matte paintings are an invaluable aid in making a film budget go further, yet they are not without their drawbacks. Richard Edlund, effects supervisor with George Lucas, confesses that the matte paintings used to portray the Cloud City of Bespin in **The Empire Strikes Back** were less than convincing. The reason is that audiences know that

although there are scores of ghostly castles in Northern Europe, cities of the future have to be created artificially.

Back projection

This is the process by which actors can be filmed driving along in an open motor car through the country without ever having to leave the studio! The technique was accidentally invented in the Twenties by Ralph Hammeras during the filming of **Divine Lady** (1929). When perfected, it involved setting up a five feet by six feet piece of clear glass which was then sprayed with frosting solution. A projection machine was placed *behind* the glass and a traveling shot from a moving car shown through it, and from such a distance that the projected picture completely covered the glass. The car was then placed in *front* of the glass screen, but far enough away from it to ensure that the lighting directed at the driver would not reach the screen, so graying the projected image. Finally, a camera was placed in front of the car and screen to shoot the composite image.

For the next 30 years, no actor ever did a dialogue scene in a car that didn't use this method. Though phoney looking and irritating, it was used by every studio from Monogram to MGM!

Far left:
A good example of just how bad back projection can look when abused at the hands of low-budget movie makers. As with the scenes in **King Kong** (1933) which combined live actors with giant monsters, this scene from **The Beast From 20,000 Fathoms** (1953) has an animated monster back-projected into a screen while live actors fire blank rounds at the screen. The end result might have looked fine in 1933, but didn't really satisfy audiences 20 years later.

Below far left:
In this scene from the daddy of all monster movies **King Kong** (1933), there are several special effects in operation. The figure of Kong is actually an 18-inch high model, fully jointed and animated against a miniature background by the stop-motion method. This footage of the tiny Kong is then back-projected onto a large screen. The figure of Fay Wray is real and is photographed against the screen to make it look as though she is being menaced by the giant ape.

Left:
During the hunt for the abducted Fay Wray in **King Kong** (1933) one of the sailors is chased up a tree by a hungry dinosaur. The dinosaur in this picture is actually a tiny model, animated for the camera by the inventor of stop motion, Willis O'Brien, then projected onto a large screen behind the actor and his tree stump.

Overleaf:
Art imitates life imitating art. . . Horror-movie masks as disguises for criminals and deviants are just as popular on-screen as off. This maniac terrorizing a small town is from **Halloween II** (1981), Rick Rosenthal's less than adequate follow-up to John Carpenter's brilliant shocker, which had made a star of Jamie Lee Curtis.

Overleaf right:
Tron (1982) was the video equivalent of **Fantastic Voyage** (1966); instead of exploring a human body, Jeff Bridges dared the dangers of a computer's circuits.

21

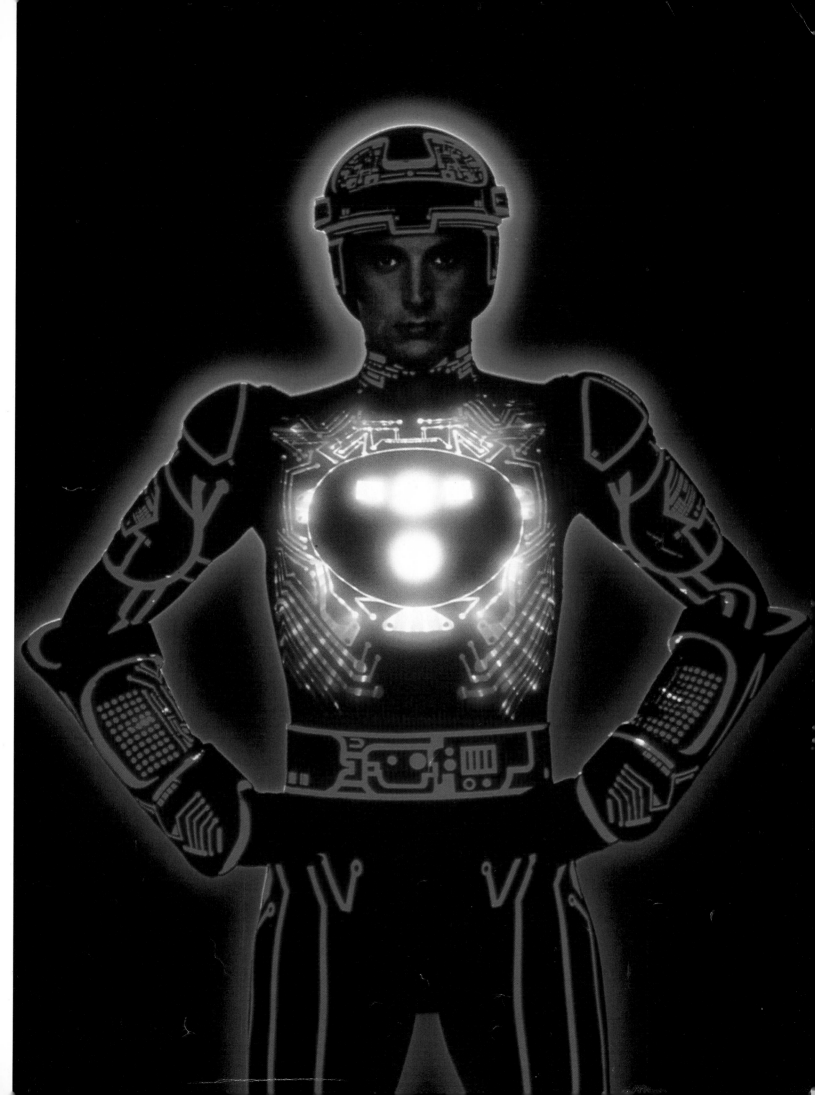

Front projection

Front projection is used in many contexts in movie making. The most obvious applications are as a substitute for back projection, with model animation, and in conjunction with matte. Its earliest major use was in **2001: A Space Odyssey** (1968), for the opening shots of apes learning how to use tools. More dramatic examples of this technique were seen in **Superman the Movie** (1978), though the film was not without its production difficulties. To begin with, Superman (actor Christopher Reeve) had to be supported off the ground in front of the front projection screen. Wires could not be used, so a small hole was cut in the screen. A steel pole, supported behind the screen by sturdy scaffolding, passed through it to a molded body harness in front of the screen. Superman was strapped into the harness and suspended there for countless hours of special-effects filming.

Using special zoom lenses, Superman could be made to appear to fly towards and away from the camera without actually moving the actor or camera.

Superman flies high above the imaginary city of Metropolis (the film makers actually used New York in **Superman the Movie**, 1978). While it might have been easier to hoist actor Christopher Reeve on a wire hundreds of feet above the city, the insurance companies would never have allowed it. So the "Zoptic Process" was developed. Basically, this consists of a front projection set-up, with Reeve suspended on a pole in front of the screen. The pole is behind Reeve in the picture extending away from us into the screen on which we can see the cityscape. That way it's hidden from the audience.

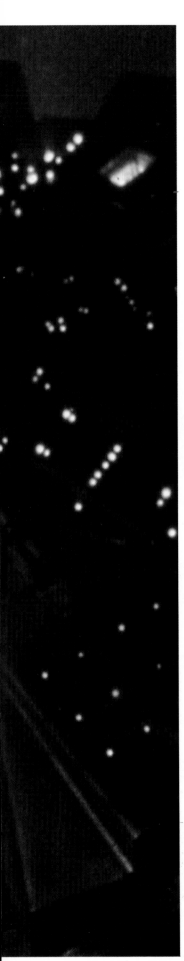

Left:
A remarkable special effects scene from Ridley Scott's **Blade Runner** (1982). Both the cityscape and the tiny spinner (flying car) are models, but instead of being filmed together in one "pass" of the camera, the spinner is filmed against a blue screen then matted into a "plate" (a still photo) of the required background.

Below:
Two actors sit on a rug, suspended before a blue screen on wires. This set-up enables special effects technicians to produce a traveling matte of the actors and carpet and thus superimpose them against any kind of background.

Traveling matte

As explained in the section on stationary matte, a matte is a device to block out a portion of a film image. In stationary matting, the matte does not move, in the traveling matte technique it does.

Imagine that you want to superimpose the image of a spaceship on a starry background. If you simply combined the film of the space ship with the film of the starry background you would end up with a spaceship filled with shining stars. To make the ship appear solid, you would have to make a spaceship-shaped hole in the starry background. However, the hole would have to move around in exact synchronization with the movement of the ship. To make this hole one uses a traveling matte.

There are several ways of creating such traveling mattes. The oldest – and, some insist, the best – way of accomplishing that task is to hand-paint hundreds of ship-silhouettes onto a strip of film. This costly process was used as recently as 1968 for the space sequences in **2001**.

Motion control

The traveling matte system was only one technique used for creating the spaceship dogfight scenes for **Star Wars** and just about every other space movie made since.

The brief given to special effects supervisor John Dykstra by **Star Wars** director George Lucas, was that the spaceship battle sequences should look as though they were filmed from a ship participating in the fight. This meant that the technicians had to devise a way around the traditional look of spaceship scenes where the camera remained in one position and dutifully recorded everything the effects men pushed in front of it. **2001** is an example of this static camera style.

The **Star Wars** technicians ingeniously solved the problem by creating a system in which the model spaceship stayed still while the camera moved. A further refinement meant that the camera moves were controlled by a computer which also enabled each precise movement to be recorded. The camera could be made to pan, tilt and track in any direction and, if need be, repeat the motions precisely for a second take. This innovative technique meant that every element, the ship, planet, explosion and starry background, could be recorded individually then combined on one piece of film to make up the finished scene.

For filming, the spaceship models were mounted on rigid pylons coated with a blue-screen material to render them invisible to the camera. The image of the ship was recorded on VistaVision, which passes through the camera horizontally instead of vertically and gives a 70mm size frame on 35mm gauge film. This larger image size meant that clarity could be maintained through several duplications.

Left:
Special effects supervisor Richard Edlund checks a model of a Star Destroyer used in **The Empire Strikes Back** (1980) before photographing it in front of a blue screen. Once this scene has been filmed, any background the film makers choose can be superimposed into the blue area with a minimum amount of fuss. In this kind of effects work it is far easier to move the camera than it is to move the model. So the spaceship is mounted on a rigid pole and the camera moves, controlled by computer so that every move can be repeated exactly if needed.

Left:
A new special effects system was developed to film the spaceship scenes in **Star Wars** (1977). This had to be capable of photographing dynamic action scenes using models. Earlier movie spaceship scenes had always been filmed at a ponderous pace, like those in **2001: A Space Odyssey** (1968). For **Star Wars**, the models were set on rigid poles in front of blue screens, while the camera was mobile. An illusion of movement was produced equally well and kept the process simple. The rocket exhausts in this picture were added later by the cel animation technique.

John Dykstra was awarded an Oscar for developing this system and a separate Oscar for the effects achieved on **Star Wars**. The "Dykstraflex" system, as it was christened, has been much copied by others. The Disney production of **The Black Hole** (1980) used a system called "aces" for its lavish motion control work. **The Empire Strikes Back**, on which Dykstra did not work, used a set-up called, cheekily, "Empireflex". Yet no matter what the process is called, if it had not been for the work of John Dykstra, all spaceship shots would still look as static as those in **2001**.

The optical printer
Optical printing is the process by which two or more pieces of film can be combined (or composited) onto a single strip of film. The technique is used specifically when film makers want to superimpose one filmed image on top of another.

The optical printer, the device used for such compositing, was invented by Linwood Dunn around 1930, and was used extensively on **King Kong**. This earliest kind of optical printer consisted of a camera set face-to-face opposite a single projector. This enabled the special effects people to rephotograph footage with the added facility of zooming in, freeze framing and step-printing, which is a process whereby the speed of the action is doubled by printing every other frame of the film. With the addition of a second projector, the optical printer really came into its own. Technicians could now combine, or superimpose two pieces of film simultaneously.

Almost every optical photographic effect in existence relies on the optical printer. The effects created in this way include such well-known "tricks" as superimposition of titles over action; lap-dissolves, where one scene fades into another; every type of optical wipe, where one scene wipes out across the screen as another scene wipes on; and split screen work, when two separate scenes are shown simultaneously on two sides of the screen.

Mechanical effects
Mechanical effects have changed very little since the earliest days of film, and remain resolutely "low-tech" in the face of computerized advances in optical effects. Yet without mechanical effects, many of the cinema's greatest scenes could never have been filmed. There would be no Yoda in **The Empire Strikes Back**, no monster in **Alien**, no grisly, on-screen bullet hits in **Bonnie and Clyde** (1967) or **The Godfather** (1971), and no rain, snow or wind in just about any movie you care to mention.

Miniatures
Short of finding or building the extravagant sets or scenery required for a cinema epic, scaled-down miniatures are the only alternative to glass or matte paintings. Miniatures have been used almost since the beginning of the movies in this way. For example, the spectacular city of Rome in both the 1926 and 1959 versions of **Ben Hur** was a miniature, as was the awesome city in **Metropolis** (1926). And in 1930,

Left:
A superb miniature of New York, circa 1980, as envisaged by the makers of **Just Imagine** (1930). Pioneering special effects technician Ralph Hammeras earned an Oscar nomination for his work on this movie, not really a science-fiction picture, but a musical fantasy.

Bottom left:
A dramatic scene from the closing moments of **Dragonslayer** (1981). The dragon is an articulated stop-motion puppet controlled, through rods, by computerized servo-motors. The background, looking just like a cloudy sky, is actually white paint dropped into a large water tank, then photographed with a movie camera. The lightning effects are cel animated – hand-drawn on clear acetate cels, animated and superimposed over the combined scene of the puppet dragon and water-tank skies.

Below:
Danny Kaye was always at his best when performing a double act with himself! He used this gimmick in several movies including **Wonder Man** (1945), **On the Riviera** (1951) and here in **On the Double** (1962). The effect of two Danny Kayes was achieved by filming Kaye twice on the same set and joining the two halves of film together using an optical printer. For scenes where Kaye had to walk past himself or shake hands with himself, tricks impossible with the double exposure method, another actor was used as a double.

Ralph Hammeras, who had invented stationary mattes and back projection, earned his second Oscar nomination for his miniature cityscape for the film **Just Imagine** (1930). The final shots of the cityscape even show flowing traffic, airplanes and dirigibles flying through the air, and all controlled by a maze of belts and pulleys concealed beneath the miniature streets.

Fifty years later, model-maker Greg Jein was using similar techniques to create some of the settings for **Close Encounters of the Third Kind**. The first miniature built by Jein for that movie resembled a stretch of Indiana countryside, over which a flight of UFOs performed a display of aerobatics. It took about six weeks to build. Jein also built the miniature highway tollbooth through which the smaller flying saucers pass, a miniature of the Devil's Tower which was replaced in the final movie by a matte painting, and the mothership itself. Originally, this was conceived as a big black shape, but director Steven Spielberg decided that he wanted a space ship that resembled an oil refinery at night. Jein's imaginative work provided stunningly successful results. However, if you

look closely enough you will see that Jein added a few comic touches to the model spaceship. As well as a silhouette of Mickey Mouse in one of the windows, there is a shark chasing some frogmen, a little R2-D2 from **Star Wars**, some World War Two fighter planes and a Volkswagen bus!

Such close attention to detail also figured prominently in Jein's miniatures for the comedy **1941** (1979). The film featured, in two amazing special effects set-pieces, miniatures of the Ocean Park funfair and Hollywood Boulevard. Jein and his team spent six months on the model funfair building arcades, food stores and buildings crammed with furniture – the model makers had put objects behind every window, the hotels had venetian blinds, and they even made pool tables and coats to hang on the walls. Only ten percent of all this work was ever seen on the screen, but the makers considered it worthwhile since some of their work did appear in close-up.

Although a matte painting could have been used to create this effect, it would have been completely useless when it came to the scene in which the funfair explodes sky-high!

Below left:
In this behind-the-scenes picture, Ray Harryhausen, effects director and co-producer of **Clash of the Titans** (1981), lines up a shot on a miniature set. **Clash of the Titans** was filmed with three times the budget of the average Harryhausen movie but, in the final analysis, was rather a disappointment. Techniques that had worked well enough for **King Kong** in 1933 now appeared hopelessly dated.

Below:
The special effects crew of **One From the Heart** (1982) photograph a miniature of Las Vegas. The makers of the film decided to do without locations and make the entire movie on a sound stage, even the exteriors. The idea was to get back to the original style of Hollywood film making of the Forties. The final result was dreamy and fake-looking, an effect the director claimed he was aiming for.

For **The Man With the Golden Gun** (1974), the villain, played by Christopher Lee, has to escape from James Bond in a car which suddenly turns into a jet aircraft. Special effects technicians under the supervision of miniature expert Derek Meddings built a model of the jet-powered flying car, the scale of which can be seen here (*left*). When seen from a distance, this comparatively large model seems quite convincing (*right*). The main picture shows Lee at the controls of a full-sized mock-up of the car. When the two pictures are intercut with each other in the film, the overall effect fools audiences into thinking Lee really does fly away in a Ford Concorde!

Wire work

Wire work, which has its origins in string puppetry, is used by special effects technicians to make objects or people seem as if they are defying gravity. For example, all of Superman's outdoor takeoffs and landings were accomplished by wire work. And when the police car in **Blade Runner** (1982) takes off in a cloud of exhaust vapor, it's a full-size, lightweight mock-up hoisted into the air by a crane.

When it comes to making actors fly, the commonest method is to use double wires attached to the actor at hip level, which is usually the center of gravity for the human body. And, unlike the version of wire flying which relies on a single wire attached to the small of the back, the hip method means that the actor only spins around when the technicians want him to.

Colin Chilvers, the special effects man responsible for "flying" Christopher Reeve in **Superman the Movie,** explained that there are some inherent problems in the wire system. To begin with, the wire has to be sufficiently strong (and therefore thick) to support the actor's weight, which of course makes it difficult to conceal. The type of wire chosen also depends on the type of background being used, how high the actor will be hoisted and what movements he will need to make. The biggest problem with wires is starting and stopping the actor, since he requires sufficient space to run up for the "launch", and room to decelerate at the other end. This reason and the fact that wires are difficult to work around corners, are why Superman's wire flying was kept to an absolute minimum.

Left:
A police "Spinner" takes to the acid rain-drenched skies in **Blade Runner** (1982). This was achieved by hoisting a full-size lightweight mock-up into the air using wires. If you examine the picture very carefully, you just may be able to make out the cables supporting the flying car.

Bottom left:
Is it a bird? Is it a plane? It's Christopher Reeve as the star of **Superman III** (1983) flying low over a car breakers' yard with the aid of wires. Careful examination of the picture may just reveal the steel cables used to hold Reeve 20 feet off the ground, but you have to look hard. All outdoor and take-off/landing shots of Reeve's flying were achieved using wires. Luckily, these were few and the majority of the flying shots used a variation on the front projection method christened the "Zoptic Process" by its inventor Zoran Perisic.

Right:
They fly through the air with the greatest of ease . . . the stuntmen in **It's a Mad, Mad, Mad, Mad World** (1963), double for characters falling off a collapsing fire-escape.

Overleaf left:
The machine that gives Jane Fonda the thrill of a lifetime in **Barbarella**, Roger Vadim's tongue-in-cheek 1967 fantasy. Luckily she is more experienced and resistant than previous victims and overtaxes the machine to destruction point.

Overleaf right:
The car that comes dangerously to life in **Christine** (1983), an unusual exercise in "animating" a full-size vehicle.

The elements

When you have millions of investors' dollars riding on a film production, unpredictability is the last thing you need – yet that is probably the most accurate word for describing the weather. Consequently, when movie makers need rain, they don't work their schedules around weather forecasts, they call in the effects man. In any event, real rain doesn't *look* like real rain on film; the best movie rain comes out of a hose pipe. Water will do, but it helps if you add something to make the liquid a little more opaque . . . like milk or white paint.

The most obvious way of creating wind is to rely on a couple of large aircraft propellers just out of camera range. Although they make a dreadful amount of noise, the dialogue is not drowned out since the soundrack for such a scene is dubbed in later. Good examples of wind and rain effects occur during the finale of **Poltergeist** (1982), which had Jobeth Williams tearing around outside the haunted house, braving the storm in a football shirt.

Snow is usually simulated by showering actors with ground-up, expanded polystyrene, while snow on the ground is faked using salt. Unfortunately, salt promotes rust so the technicians have to be very careful about keeping their equipment well away. For the special effect scenes on the ice planet in **The Empire Strikes Back** the effects crew used baking soda, instead of salt, which seemed to work satisfactorily.

Fog is one of the great cinematic devices. It enhanced just about every Hollywood horror movie during the Forties, as well as making a major appearance every time Hollywood portrayed London. The fog used in movies is produced by a little "black box", the fog machine. It produces choking noxious gas which is released by a simple trigger device. The other type of fog seen in the movies, often used in swamp scenes, clings to the ground and is generated by dropping a couple of chunks of "dry ice" – frozen carbon dioxide – into water.

When fire is featured in movies, it is necessary to call in the experts. Fire is difficult, if not impossible, to fake convincingly, so real fire must be used during shooting. A film like **The Towering Inferno** (1974) was a nightmare for the effects people. To achieve convincing end results and keep the fire safely under control at all times, piping was run all over the sets and connected up to a supply of propane gas. In this way, the fire could be turned on and off at will.

Left:
In this scene from **Raiders of the Lost Ark** (1981), the fire on the non-inflammable set is achieved by smearing a flammable paste on everything that has to be seen to burn before touching it off with a match. All sorts of problems were experienced by the crew during this crucial scene, including a moment when the fire got so out of hand that it set fire to the rafters in the roof of the studio. Fortunately, the adequate precautions meant that at no point was the fire ever dangerously out of control.

Right:
A real Han Solo (actor Harrison Ford) sitting on a fake Taun Taun in **The Empire Strikes Back** (1980). For the long shots, both rider and mount were animated, articulated models, operated by animation expert Phil Tippett. The dummy Taun Taun was fitted with piping in its nostrils so that the steam of its "breath" could be seen as a cloud in the sub-zero air of the Norwegian location.

Bullets and explosions

In the good old days of Hollywood, the only way to get bullet hits and explosions on screen was to use real bullets and explosions. In films like **G Men** (1935), with James Cagney, the hail of lead you saw peppering window frames around the hero's head was actually being fired by an off-camera sharp-shooter. Within a couple of years, however, the Screen Actors Guild stepped in to protest and the practice was promptly discontinued.

In modern-day gangster movies, like **The Godfather** and **Bonnie and Clyde**, bullet hits on inanimate objects were simulated by a very simple process: the effects crew drilled holes where they wanted the bullets to explode; they then pushed a small explosive charge, called a "squib", into the hole, and attached the detonation wires; finally, they plugged up the hole with putty or wax, painting over the material to camouflage it from the camera. The subsequent explosion could be guaranteed to leave a very convincing bullet hole.

A similar technique is used when actors have to be shot. First, a metal plate is taped to the actor's skin, which protects them when the squib is detonated. The squib itself is attached to the plate and over this is placed a small plastic envelope filled with fake blood (the methods of making fake blood are covered in the

section on makeup). The actor then puts on his costume over this assembly. As with other types of bullet hits, the squib is detonated by connecting it to a battery. The resulting effect on screen is bloodily effective, if a little stomach-churning.

The squib technique works just as well for simulating hits from laser pistols, a common request from movie directors of science fiction. The squib is rigged in the normal way, the actor with the blaster aims and fires and the effects man sets off the squib. Later, the optical effects people animate the laser ray onto this piece of film, working backwards from the squib detonation to ensure that the whole effect is timed perfectly.

Above:
Barbara Hershey suffers from indoor lightning at the hands of **The Entity** (1982). The lightning effects are produced using simple cel animation and are superimposed onto the footage of Hershey reacting via the optical printer. Regular lightning in the sky is also usually imitated in movies by this method.

Right:
The Godfather (1972): As Sonny Corleone (James Caan) climbs from the car, the machine gun bullets thud into his body and into the metal panels of the car. If you look carefully, you can see the wire leading out of Caan's trouser leg to the control panel where the "bullet hits" are controlled by an effects technician.

Exploding spaceships present a very different kind of problem. For the scenes in **The Empire Strikes Back** in which the ships disintegrate in mid-air, special effects supervisor Richard Edlund rented an armory in San Francisco, the largest single room he could find in the area. The team constructed their own black ceiling, approximately 100 feet by 60 feet, and photographed a series of explosions just below it using high-speed cameras.

By shooting the explosions from below, the blast debris seemed to defy gravity, scattering evenly in all directions. They were then superimposed over doomed spacecraft using the optical printer.

Left:
A devastating explosion from **Blue Thunder** (1983). For detonations of this nature, the effects technicians have to strive for maximum visual effect with the minimum amount of dangerous explosives.

Above:
A dynamic scene from **The Blue Max** (1966). The bodies flying through the air, each in several pieces, are not real. These are dummies (not very good ones) piled on top of an explosive charge – which *is* real – and flung into the air by the

blast. But as the film rolls in a cinema or on television the glimpse we get of the explosion and the flying bodies is just quick enough to make us think that we are watching real men flying through the air. The trick works only if you don't see it too well.

Puppetry

Modern puppets are very complex pieces of machinery and were used most stunningly in **Alien**. However, the "chest burster", the young version of the creature that bursts out of John Hurt's body as he's eating a plate of spaghetti, is nothing more than an elaborate hand puppet, manipulated by its builder, Roger Dicken. In order to create this effect, Dicken lay on a trolley under the meal table, the puppet was passed up through a split in the table and through a false chest attached to Hurt's neck. The camera then cut, showing the creature fleeing rapidly across the floor — Dicken, trolley and miniature alien were all pulled fiercely along on a piece of rope. The monster's tail even lashed about as it fled across the tabletop, scattering dishes behind. Dicken explains that this realistic effect was achieved by inserting a tube inside the tail, and connecting it to a compressed air bottle. When the air was turned on, the tail (securely taped to Dicken's hand) "thrashed around".

Although the large adult form of the alien was played in long shots by 6 feet 10 inches tall Bolaji Badejo, the head of the creature was a complicated mechanical puppet built by Carlo Rambaldi. Rambaldi had been brought to Hollywood from his native Italy by producer Dino De Laurentiis to build the full-size Kong for the remake version of **King Kong** (1976). As it turned out, the Kong seen in the movie was mostly Rick Baker in a superb ape suit, because Rambaldi's robot didn't work. But Rambaldi redeemed himself when he created Puck, the smiling alien seen in the closing moments of **Close Encounters of the Third Kind**. It took 15 cables to operate each movement;

Below:
This is the weird baby that was the villain of the horror film **It's Alive** (1974). The dummy baby was built by Oscar-winning makeup man Rick Baker, who later worked on **An American Werewolf in London** (1981).

Right:
Christopher Tucker (in foreground) and his crew bring the skinless dummy of actor Stephen Rea to life for **The Company of Wolves** (1984). The dummy's several movements are controlled through cables.

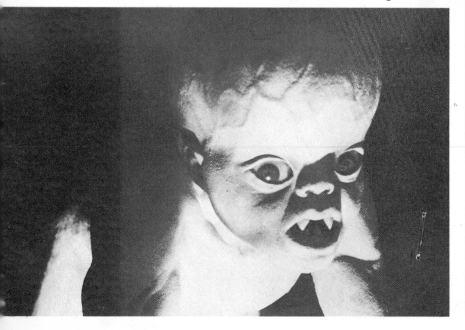

Left:
Werewolves, out of fashion for decades, took on a new lease of life in the Eighties. The Irish director of **The Company of Wolves** (1984), Neil Jordan, co-wrote the script with novelist Angela Carter to create a tingling Freudian version of the Red Riding Hood story.

Below:
In this grisly scene from **Dragonslayer** (1981) a baby dragon enjoys a light snack of dead princess. Of course the princess (Chloe Salaman) isn't really dead and that isn't really a baby dragon. It's fake blood and a rather clever hand puppet. But with this puppet, the

jaws are properly hinged, the eyes blink and the nostrils flare. The puppet's operator is safely out of sight of the camera, concealed beneath the fake rock on which the princess lies.

seven to create the facial expressions and another five to produce the arm and hand movements. Esophagus and chest movements were accomplished by pumping air from cylinders in through tubes. Rambaldi also contributed intricate mechanical puppets for **E.T. The Extra-Terrestrial** – though some scenes were shot with midget actors in rubber suits.

Larger and more elaborate kinds of puppets were the full-size sharks built for the 1975 Steven Spielberg blockbuster, **Jaws**. Spielberg managed to contract veteran mechanical-effects wizard Bob Mattey to build the three full-sized sharks needed for the production. (Mattey had previously built the full-size squid puppet, which had tried to eat James Mason in the Disney spectacular, **20,000 Leagues Under the Sea** (1954).) One shark was pulled through the water on a kind of sled, guided by submerged divers who also worked the beast's fins and tail. The other two versions of "Bruce", as he was affectionately called

by the crew, were in fact just the sides of a shark, one designed to be filmed from the left and one from the right. These sharks ran on a kind of underwater railway for 60 feet, connected to the track by a pivot arm which enabled the sharks to dive, surface, swim and generally look menacing.

But what really made the various versions of "Bruce" convincing was the skin, developed by plastics expert and mechanical effects maestro Roy Arboghast. Arboghast was hired to work on **Jaws** primarily to create a realistic fake shark skin for Mattey's full-size puppets. He set up an experimental section of shark, about six feet long, complete with the ribs and mechanics. Skins of various types, including latex and urethane, were tried in order to find a material that would stand the strain of the shark's movements without tearing and that wouldn't need to be repaired after the complete model had been submerged in water.

Left:
A remarkable scene from
Twilight Zone the Movie
(1983) in which Kevin
McCarthy pulls a rabbit from
a hat. The grotesque bunny
is a sophisticated
mechanical puppet,
operated from off-screen by
effects technicians. Weird
lighting makes the moment
particularly eerie.

Above:
In **Royal Wedding** (1951),
Fred Astaire is seen to dance
up the wall, across the
ceiling and down the other
wall all in one take – no
camera cuts! No wires were
used and no mirrors, either.
The camera is attached to
the set and the set is
mounted on an axle so that
it can be rotated.

The last word

Whenever you try to break down an inexact science like special effects into categories, there's always something that steadfastly defies classification. In this case, it's the dynamic effect seen in **Royal Wedding** (1951) when Fred Astaire dances into a room. Nothing unusual in that, it seems, until he dances up the wall, across the ceiling and down the other wall in one shot! The trick was so successful that Kubrick used the idea in **2001: A Space Odyssey** when the stewardess on board the Pan-Am moon clipper pulls the same stunt. Director Tobe Hooper employed the same technique in **Poltergeist** when a victim of the mysterious forces of the Other World falls up the wall and across the ceiling of her bedroom. All three directors resorted to the same trick. The actors stayed where they were and the room (and the cameras) *rotated* around them. Simple but effective – like all the best special effects.

Of course, when the end credits roll, it's not really so important how the effects were done, but whether the audience believe in them. And to believe in the special effects, audiences have to believe in the characters, whether they are blown to the ends of outer space or vaporized by laser beams. In short, special effects, no matter how ingenious, are no substitute for good stories and good acting.

51

THE GREAT STUNTS

In the early days of filming, before the stuntman was a recognized artist, lesser stars were expected to do many of their own feats of daring. Thus Eileen Sedgwick can be seen venturing onto a narrow plank apparently high above the city of Los Angeles in the serial **Terror Trail** (1921). Actually a rooftop terrace is less than 20 feet below her.

It can safely be said that no cycle of films has enjoyed a greater popularity or a longer run than those based on the James Bond novels. In the near quarter of a century that has elapsed since he first strode across our cinema screens, the character of Bond, no matter who plays him, has been a winner with filmgoers everywhere. Certainly no series of films has grossed more money at the box office.

Each new production commands a larger budget, bigger stars and more exotic locations than the last. But the secret for this continued success is rooted in the appeal of Bond himself, the glamor of the backgrounds, the obvious charms of the Bond girls and, the main contributing factor, the fantastic action. No doubt author Ian Fleming would find the character he created in 1953 difficult to compare with the James Bond on the screen.

The fact remains, however, that the public adores this superspy for his feats of daring and action. Why? Perhaps it's because secretly they know that no matter how many gory deaths they see, how many battalions of machine-gun waving villains are shot down, or how many individual bodies are blown through windows, blasted off balconies, or burned alive – at the end of the shot when the film's director calls "cut!", they are all going to get to their feet, dust themselves off and await instructions for the next set-up – because they are all *stuntmen*.

Strict supervision

Novelist Raymond Chandler once said: "When you don't know what to do next in a story, have someone come through the door with a gun in his hand." The same can be said of a Bond film. When the plot line is sagging, throw in a fight or a stunt. The Bond films have made use of everything from the ejector seat in his Lotus Elan in **Goldfinger** (1964) to the individual jet-propelled back pack that enables him to make his escape during the pre-credits sequence in **Thunderball** (1965), and the Union Jack canopied parachute in **The Spy Who Loved Me** (1977). He has had fist fights in railway compartments, in elevators, on cable cars and the roofs of moving trains, and even underwater.

Most of these action-packed scenes have been carried out, in part at least, by the artist playing Bond himself, but always, it must be stressed, under the strict supervision of a team of specialists, headed by a stunt co-ordinator. It is their job to see that our hero carries out the mayhem with conviction but without danger to himself and those around him. There have been exceptions, but on the whole their work is

53

successful. An example of this can be seen in **Never Say Never Again** (1983), when Bond, with the heroine seated behind him, leaps a horse 70 feet off the walls of an East African stronghold where they've been held prisoner, into the sea below. Moviegoers all over the world were up in arms over this scene.

In some countries the shot of the horse and its riders landing in the water was cut. But why? If Bond fans are prepared to accept that the overturning of cars and motorbikes can be achieved without mishap to those involved, will they not accept that the same experts will take every precaution to ensure the well-being of an animal who puts his trust in them?

In fact, so much attention was given to the animal that three weeks preparation was spent just getting the horse used to sea water prior to the sequence being filmed, and the first attempt to do the stunt had to be called off because the stunt co-ordinator was not satisfied that the safety stipulations laid down by him had been satisfactorily adhered to. The team looked after the horse so well that, far from suffering any ill effects, it continued to swim around quite happily for ten minutes after the cameras had ceased to roll.

Vastly underrated

Back in the early days of the cinema the stuntman was a shadowy figure on the periphery of the industry, capable of being described in the press as "a kind of insane daredevil, who would take a chance on anything if the thrill was big enough and the reward sufficient to buy him another bottle of booze". Now he is a highly paid specialist, sometimes earning far in excess of other film personnel per day.

In the definitive work on the silent film era, *The Parade's Gone By* (Secker & Warburg, 1968), Kevin Brownlow quotes veteran stuntman "Suicide" Buddy Mason on the type of qualifications required of a stuntman in the Twenties. Mason ironically pointed out that . . . "When you get so they call you by your first name when you come into the hospital — then you belong"! Such accidents were extremely costly to the production companies, whether they happened to the stuntmen or to the stars. If a star was injured, the cost was in lost shooting time; injury to the stuntman cost the studio in terms of bad publicity, not only with the public, but within the industry itself, where replacements might be hard to find.

An example of this bad publicity followed the death of stuntman Gene Perkins in 1924. He was killed while attempting a plane-to-train transfer down a rope ladder at 50 miles an hour. A couple of days later Paul

Australian stuntmen playing with fire in **Mad Max 2** (1981). It's lucky that director George Miller is a fully qualified medical doctor! His films have been virtually the only monster box-office hits from the Australian movie revival that flourished briefly from the mid-Seventies onward.

Right and far right:
The actress Pearl White never did a stunt in her life. A team of stuntmen in skirts carried out all the action for her **Perils of Pauline** series. In 1922, while she was making **Plunder** in New York, an inexperienced chauffeur was killed doubling for her.

Malvern, who had been standing on top of the train waiting for Perkins to swoop down for a hand-to-hand struggle, was asked by the company's production manager to dress up in the dead man's costume and jump from the top of a speeding train. He wanted to combine these shots with those of Perkin's death. Malvern, an experienced performer, for whom a leap from the roof of a speeding train held no terror, refused point blank.

The work of stuntmen in the early days was fully appreciated by neither the public nor the producers. The former assumed that for most of the dangerous stunts dummies were used, while the latter took them for granted. Perhaps the best summation of this attitude toward stunt performers comes from veteran stunt flyer Dick Grace in his book *The Squadron Of Death* (Constable, 1930). "The stars think the stuntman is just a little above an extra. The producers think he is a little below a moron. The public has never heard of him."

GETTING DOWN TO BUSINESS

Ironically, it was a woman who put the stuntmen in business. Yet Pearl White, "Queen of the Serials" or "The Lady Daredevil of the Films" as she was variously known, never did a stunt in her life. True, she did a lot of running around, was manhandled by various foreign villains, and, on one memorable occasion, was accidentally cast adrift in a gas-balloon for a couple of hours. It was probably this mishap, which occurred during the making of **The Perils of Pauline** (1914), that prompted her employers to rethink any further plans for hazardous sequences. Consequently, two ex-cowboys, Eddie Kelly and Dick Lamarr were

put on the payroll. For the next six years, kitted out in various wigs and skirts, they took her place when the script called for anything remotely dangerous. Unfortunately neither of them were on hand for the filming of **Plunder** (1922), when the action called for Pearl to leap from a moving bus to the underside of a bridge.

Director George Seitz offered the job to his chauffeur, John Stevenson. Unfortunately, Stevenson's attempt was pathetically misjudged – onlookers later claimed that in leaping upward energetically he struck his head on the edge of the bridge and, unable to hang on, fell 18 feet on to the road below. He died two days later of a cerebral hemorrhage. This was deliberately hushed up by the production company to avoid bad publicity and because the credibility of Pearl White's characters would suffer if the public found out that she didn't take part in her dangerous scenes. Her inability to perform her own stunts was cruelly unmasked when, in a Paris stage production of **The Perils of Pauline**, she found that her entrance was a "slide for life" down a cable stretching from the royal circle to the center of the stage. When the French backers of the show discovered that this and a number of other feats in the script were beyond her powers, the production was canceled.

Pearl White's successor as the "Queen of the Serials" was Ruth Roland, who didn't hide the fact that she was extensively doubled by Bob Rose, a professional aviator and wing walker, who previously stunted in Mack Sennett comedies. Bob Rose certainly qualifies as one of the first all-rounders. In addition to being an ex-army flyer and parachutist, he had earned a living as racing jockey, trick rider in the circus and motorcycle and automobile racer.

Female first

Around this time Ruth Roland's main rival was the actress Helen Holmes, who starred in the serial **The Hazards of Helen**. She enjoyed the distinction of having Helen Gibson, wife of the famous silent cowboy star "Hoot" Gibson, as the first female double to undertake her stuntwork. Gibson is undoubtedly the first stuntwoman of any note.

She began her career in 1910 as a rodeo rider; in 1911 she appeared in a number of Westerns and remained on the West coast, eking out a precarious living, until 1914, when she was signed up to double for Helen Holmes. For the next two years, and in 119 episodes which boasted such stirring titles as **The Girl at the Throttle** and **The Girl Telegrapher's Peril**, Helen Gibson did every stunt possible on and around speeding locomotive engines. These included leaping from the back of a galloping horse to a speeding engine cabin, jumping from bridges on to trains passing beneath, leaping from the footplate of a 60-mile-an-hour express to another train traveling on a parallel line, and – her best stunt of all – driving a motorbike along a station platform for a leap onto the flat-car of a passing train.

Above:
Helen Gibson rose from a stunt double for Helen Holmes to leading lady in **The Hazards of Helen**.

Right:
Helen Holmes, early rival to serial queen Pearl White, in a 1915 posed still from **The Hazards of Helen** (1914-17).

Safety equipment

It must be understood that the safety equipment used by stunt artists at this time was primitive in comparison to the equipment available today. For the D.W. Griffith film **Intolerance** (1916), trapeze artists were hired to fall into slack nets in order to capture the realism of guards falling from the walls of Babylon. Richard Talmadge dived into a couple of ordinary mattresses in the 1913 serial **The Million Dollar Mystery** and into deep sand for a later Slim Summerville comedy. Harvey Parry used a canvas safety appliance supplied by the Los Angeles fire department for a two-reeler in which he was doubling comedian Erle Fox – and bounced off it twice. Another old timer recalls seeing Eddie Kelly in full wig and skirts on a Pearl White serial, working his way hand-over-hand along an overhead wire with a large carpet 60 feet below.

THE EARLY STUNT STARS

If we accept that the stuntman was an established figure in the movies by 1914, then the **Keystone Kops** – Mack Sennett's team of crazy comedy policemen – were the worst paid stuntmen on record. Sennett avoided paying them cash adjustments for falling down flights of stairs, crashing through windows, jumping off burning roofs, leaping out of the way of speeding trains or being dragged behind careering vehicles by claiming that this was part of the salaried job.

Although they were unaware of it, the "Kops" were paving the way for "stunt stars", a new breed of film personality who enjoyed a ten-year vogue at the box office, until escalating insurance premiums and the coming of sound rendered them redundant. The scripts had little in the way of content, but made up for this with bags of action.

Houdini

Among the performers who fall into this category, only a handful are remembered today. High on the list is Harry Houdini, whose career as an illusionist and escapologist had already made him world famous in the theater and vaudeville. Billed as "The man who walks through walls" there was no denying his showmanship and mystique. On the silver screen, however, it was a different story, for his personality did not get over to the audiences. His stunting abilities were limited and most of his action had to be carried out by professional substitutes. When word got round that he had been doubled by wing walker Robert Kennedy for a plane-to-plane transfer on **The Grim Game** (1921), Houdini arrogantly tried to pretend that he hadn't been doubled by offering a reward of $1000 to any one who could prove that a stuntman had taken his place.

Although nobody came forward to disprove his claim, the public began to lose interest in him as a film star. Houdini tried to make a comeback by working entirely without doubles but, no longer in his prime, his more hazardous undertakings had to be faked and the faking was obvious. For instance, while hanging from a ledge adjacent to Niagara Falls for **The Man From Beyond** (1921) eagle-eyed movie fans were able to spot the wires leading to a harness under his jacket. In a later scene, the same harness enabled him to swim through some shallow rapids, well above the falls, far too easily. He died in 1926 at the comparatively early age of 53, when a punch to the stomach, delivered unexpectedly, led to a ruptured appendix and peritonitis.

Left:
Mack Sennett's Keystone Kops were the worst paid stuntmen in Hollywood. Sennett claimed that all the comedy stunts they had to perform were part of their characterizations and refused to adjust their salaries or give bonuses for individual gags and hazards.

Left:
Silent stunt double Jack Duffy successfully completes a rooftop leap for a Twenties Christie comedy. A gag like this would have earned him only a $5 or $10 adjustment to his basic $2 extra's daily fee.

Below:
A 1928 MGM publicity still purporting to show a contract stuntman being knocked over by a car.

"Hurricane" Hutchison

Houdini's immediate rival was Charles Hutchison, known variously as "Hutch" and "Hurricane". For the early part of his career he could honestly claim to have performed all his own stunts, albeit haphazardly. A failed actor, he had attempted to build up his stunt star image in 1918 on the strength of a doubtful reputation for performing suicidal feats on a motorcycle. This was borne out in one of his earliest film appearances for Pathé, when he attempted to jump an embankment with Edith Thornton as a pillion passenger. In what was to become almost a hallmark of most of his major stunts it went wrong, and Miss Thornton received the brunt of the damage resulting in partial facial paralysis.

Hutchison continued stunting for the next three years, causing mishap and injury to himself and those around him. While filming **Double Adventure** in 1921 an ill-conceived dive from a second story window, taken at a downward angle, resulted in two broken wrists. (An accident that was repeated with near fatal results to Burt Reynolds during the filming of **Shamus** (1972)). The accident brought about such a complete loss of nerve that his subsequent films, including **Hurricane Hutch** (1921), **Go Get 'Em Hutch** (1922), **Speed** (1923), **The Fortieth Door** (1924) and **Lightning Hutch** (1925) were achieved only with the aid of stunt doubles, who were changed from film to film as the now middle-aged performer became increasingly overweight. After 1926 he was never heard of again.

Eddie Polo

Eddie Polo deserves a mention if only for the three world records he set up in a single year, 1916. These included the first plane-to-motorboat transfer, parachuting from a height of over 4,000 feet, and leaping a horse off a 50-foot cliff.

Coming from a circus background, where he had learned acrobatic and contortionist skills, plus tight-rope walking, riding and animal handling, he possessed all the qualifications necessary to be the screen's top stunt star of that time. Unfortunately, he had a personality problem that bordered on schizophrenia. This made many of his claims suspect, particularly those concerning his noble Italian background, which at one time Universal incorporated into their publicity material. He had started out as a catcher in a circus trapeze act and then drifted into movies, first as a rider on a couple of "Broncho Billy" Anderson westerns, then taking falls in comedies for the Mack Sennett Studios. After this he was hired by Universal to appear in their serial **The Broken Coin** (1915) as stuntman and supporting artist to Grace Cunard, the production's star. Upon receiving a number of fan letters, he demanded bigger parts but was unceremoniously fired instead.

Later, he was re-hired and fired once more but, since the public liked him, he was taken on yet again. For the next five years he stunted his way through 133 serial episodes, but at a terrible cost. He was trampled on by a horse in **Bull's Eye** (1918), mauled by a lion in

King of the Circus (1920), and nearly drowned after a 40-foot fall into a lake in **The Vanishing Dagger** (1920). In 1921 he set up his own production company but few could work with him and his one independent serial, **Captain Kidd** (1922), failed disastrously at the box office.

Joe Bonomo

Another American-Italian, Joe Bonomo, became Eddie Polo's successor. After winning a "Mr. Apollo" body-building competition in New York in 1922, Bonomo was offered a contract on the Lon Chaney film, **A Light in the Dark** (1922). Believing this to be a leading character role, the youthful Bonomo accepted eagerly and did just as he was told. Doing what he was told included being a cop chasing a jewel thief down a street, then dressing up as the jewel thief and jumping into a river. Next he had to play a character who jumped off a moving train, after which he dressed up as someone else and took a punch on the jaw from Lon Chaney himself. In all, he played 20 different roles in action sequences during the course of this one film. When, in amazement, he questioned the film's director he was promptly told: "Don't worry it'll all come out OK in the cutting room."

Bonomo attended the film's New York premiere, accompanied by his family and friends, but they were all amazed to discover that, in addition to not getting his name mentioned on the film's titles, all his scenes had been taken in such long shot that his face was

Top left:
A typical publicity shot of the Silent era used to entice moviegoers to see Charles Hutchison, billed as "The Thrill-A-Minute Stunt King", in his latest serial, **Hurricane Hutch** (1921). Hutchison made his reputation doing motorcycle stunts (*left*).

Right:
Stunt star of the Twenties Joe Bonomo attempting a car-to-plane transfer. When you take into consideration that the stalling speed of an old biplane was about 55 mph, which means that flying at less than this speed involves a risk of crashing, it's safe to estimate that this stunt is being performed at 60 mph plus.

unrecognizable and other actors had been substituted in the close-ups. Far from being one of the film's leading characters, he had been tricked into doing all the hazardous sequences in the film for a fraction of the fee it would have cost to hire a team of movie stuntmen!

Such treatment made him so determined to succeed that he went to Hollywood where his first job was doubling for Lon Chaney, swinging on the cathedral bells and sliding down ropes on the 1923 version of **The Hunchback of Notre Dame**.

Richard Talmadge

During the early years of the cinema, Bonomo was in competition with another stunt star of Italian extraction, Richard Talmadge, although most stuntmen will tell you there was no contest. Talmadge was the best there was.

Born Sylvester Mazetti, Talmadge came from a village on the Italian/Swiss border to America with an acrobatic troupe. His early film work was in New York in 1913 which met with such little success that he decided, while on vacation in California, to turn to Hollywood. His fifty-year career covered just about every facet of stunting, both before the cameras as a stuntman and stunt star, and behind them as a stunt co-ordinator and second-unit director.

One of his earliest claims to fame was that he doubled for the legendary Douglas Fairbanks. Yet this boast is open to dispute, because Douglas Fairbanks Jr. has always maintained that *nobody* stood in for his father during the action sequences. What is certain, however, is that Fairbanks Sr. surrounded himself with a team of experts, both physical and technical, in order to maintain the high standard of thrills and action that were the hallmark of his films. No doubt Talmadge was one of these specialists.

For instance, if the script called for Fairbanks to climb swiftly and gracefully up a wall, Talmadge would supervise the fixing of the hidden handgrips and footholds and test them himself while Fairbanks looked on and decided with the director and cameraman which would be the best angle to film from. He would then change into costume and perform the stunt while the cameras rolled. This is standard procedure on a modern film, but in those days was quite an innovation.

Left:
Richard Talmadge – the man who could defy gravity, or so it would appear. Talmadge's ability to drop from great heights with the minimum amount of equipment to break his fall was uncanny. He once claimed to have leapt from 40 feet onto a single mattress.

Right:
Douglas Fairbanks Sr. poses for his role in **The Black Pirate** (1926), one of a string of blockbuster movies he made between 1920 and 1930.

Douglas Fairbanks Sr.

For more than a generation the name Fairbanks was synonymous with the word "stunt". Whereas the serial and comedy films first made film audiences aware of the extra dimensions that leaping and tumbling bodies added to their entertainment, it took Douglas Fairbanks to refine the antics of the stunt stars to produce a more enthralling action film.

His beginnings in Hollywood were inauspicious. He was a noted light comedian on the Broadway stage and in theaters in the East, and his first performances for Triangle Films were in mediocre westerns. Unable to fit in with the directorial style of D.W. Griffith, Fairbanks floundered for nearly five years in a series of forgettable films before helping to form United Artists in 1919.

For the next 10 years he was the world's number one stunt star, appearing in a series of adventure and action-packed films which have since become movie classics. These include **The Mark of Zorro** (1920), **The Three Musketeers** (1921), **Robin Hood** (1922), **The Thief of Bagdad** (1924), **The Black Pirate** (1926), **The Gaucho** (1927) and **The Iron Mask** (1929). In real life he was no more than medium height, stockily built, not endowed with abundant good looks, and on the verge of middle age when the first of this run of box-office blockbusters were filmed. What, then, was the secret of his success? The answer must be in the planning of each of his films. According to his son, Fairbanks Sr. and his team wouldn't just walk out on set to try a stunt. The stunts were choreographed on paper and then rehearsed, before the specially-designed sets were built to accomodate the carefully prepared moves.

With this immense dedication to perfection, he learned to use a seventeenth-century rapier in an authentic manner, crack a bull-whip expertly, and pitch a South American bola with skill and dexterity. Much of his skill was aided by the innovative talent of his brother, Robert. It was he who designed such contrivances as a chute concealed in a huge drape which allowed Fairbanks to escape from his pursuers by apparently sliding down an enormous ornamental curtain in **Robin Hood** (1922); a series of mini-trampolines hidden in huge vases, eight feet tall, for Fairbanks to bounce in and out of in **The Thief of Bagdad** (1924); and a system that enabled the star to plunge his dagger into the topmost sail of a galleon and slide 24 feet down to the mizzen-deck for **The Black Pirate** (1926).

However, the writer Anita Loos remembers one occasion when the fearless star of a thousand stunts had to admit defeat and call in a double. It occured during the filming of a scene where Fairbanks had to deflate an ordinary car tire with a lady's hat-pin. He bungled every take and, finally, to everyone's amazement confessed that he was frightened of being blinded should the tire explode. He couldn't do the shot and a stuntman was brought in.

There is another interesting Fairbanks anecdote, this time concerning **Robin Hood** (1922). The insurance companies refused to cover Fairbanks for a hand-over-hand climb up the 80-foot chains supporting the drawbridge to the castle. Consequently a stunt

double was brought in and did a successful "take", but Fairbanks complained and insisted that someone with more agility should be used on a re-take. Shooting was suspended while calls went out for a competent replacement.

Fairbanks disappeared and the technicians and crew settled down to wait. Suddenly, the director Allan Dwan became aware of a figure in the Robin Hood costume climbing nimbly up the drawbridge chain and ordered the cameras to roll. As the lone figure continued to ascend the huge edifice in record time, the unit cheered on the unknown stuntman in sheer admiration. Dwan, naturally, wanted to know who the man was and, as if on cue, the intrepid performer turned and flashing his famous smile revealed that it was none other than Fairbanks himself!

Comedy stunts

The two names that invariably come to mind when anyone mentions stunting in the Twenties are Buster Keaton and Harold Lloyd. Keaton's stunting abilities are in a class of their own, as all his films were built entirely around visual jokes. He is only known to have used a double once during this time. It was during the filming of **College** (1927), when the script called for him to execute a pole vault through a second story window into a bedroom. For this he hired Lee Barnes, the U.S. and Olympic pole vault champion, because Keaton believed quite rightly that if you wanted a job done properly then you must get the right man.

Keaton was an acknowledged expert on knockabout tumbling, having started in vaudeville with the family act *The Three Keatons* under the sub-billing: "The Human Mop". During the course of the 17-minute act he was systematically dumped and thrown all over the stage by his father, who then launched him through the scenery into the wings before finally bouncing him off the bass drum in the orchestra pit! At one performance, Keaton alleges, his father actually threw him at a young man in the audience who had passed an uncomplimentary remark about Mrs. Keaton's saxophone playing.

67

Although Keaton could claim that all of his film stunts were performed by himself and no other, it was at a terrible cost. The personal injuries he lists in his biography, *My Wonderful World of Slapstick*, reveal a broken right leg that took four months to heal, water on both elbows, and a broken neck that he was unaware of at the time it happened. Why did Keaton subject himself to such punishment at a time when most of the other stars were happy to let professional stuntmen take the risks for them? The answer lies in the fact that as a performer, Keaton was a real professional and unique.

The "human fly"

Harold Lloyd's best remembered film is probably **Safety Last** (1923) in which he has to climb up the side of a large department store as a publicity stunt. Lloyd based the scenario for this film on Bill Strothers, a contemporary and popular personality otherwise known as the "human fly". He so impressed Lloyd

that he called him in as technical advisor and stunt double on the famous comedy. The "human fly", who appears in the film as himself, was on call for three weeks, with little or nothing to do. Strothers therefore asked to be released for a morning, but while climbing the face of a high building he slipped and fell and had to be hospitalized. As a result, Harold Lloyd performed the entire climbing sequence himself.

In a later film, **Feet First** (1932), he was doubled for most of the shots on the exteriors of a high building by Harvey Parry, who was sworn to secrecy for the next 50 years. Nevertheless, the parts of the climb that Lloyd did perform himself are all the more remarkable for the fact that he had only two usable fingers on his right hand, the other two having been blown off in 1919 when a dummy bomb he was holding for a publicity still exploded. The other little known fact that makes Lloyd's climbing feats even more amazing is that the star was a life-long sufferer of chronic vertigo!

Far left:
Safety Last (1923) put Harold Lloyd on the map as a comedy stunt star. He was inspired to make the film by watching the antics of a "human fly" climbing the side of a building in downtown Los Angeles and hired him to act as technical advisor and double on the film. However, the "human fly" became injured so Lloyd did all the stunts himself.

Left:
Harold Lloyd's new variation on an old theme in **Feet First** (1932). Nearly a decade after his masterpiece **Safety Last** (1923), Lloyd was once again hanging crazily from dizzy heights. Filmgoers can have no conception of what agony it must have been for him to have worked on these films. For a sufferer of chronic vertigo, performing at heights of up to 100 or 150 feet, with only a mattress covered platform 15 feet below, must have seemed terrifying. Legend has it that when filming was completed the crew dropped a dummy onto this supposed safety rig to see how effective it was. The dummy bounced off and crashed down into the street below!

69

"YAKIMA" CANUTT

Stagecoach (1939) contains one of the most admired cinema stunts ever made. As the pursuing Indian warriors gallop alongside the team of horses pulling the stagecoach, one of them suddenly leaps from the back of his pony on to the leading pair and proceeds to try and cut them loose. Sitting on the roof of the coach is John Wayne, who blasts a couple of shots from his Winchester at the struggling figure. The Indian, when hit, instead of taking the traditional and safe sideways fall from the back of the horse, falls between the pounding hooves of the galloping team and is dragged for what seems half a mile before releasing his grip, so allowing the six horses and the stagecoach to pass over him. And to ensure that the audience is under no illusion that this was performed by a stuntman and not a dummy, the dazed Indian rolls over and over, before getting to his feet. This remarkable feat of action was performed by the incredible "Yakima" Canutt.

The debt of gratitude that is owed by filmgoers and filmmakers alike to Canutt was repaid, in part at least, at the 1967 Academy Awards Ceremony, when he was presented with a special Oscar for his services to the industry. Sadly, his contribution to screen action had gone unremarked for almost half a century.

Edward Enos Canutt, to give him his real name, was born in 1895 on a small ranch in the Snake River Hills of Washington State. He earned the nickname "Yakima" 17 years later at the start of his very successful career on the rodeo circuit where he was world champion bronc rider and all-round cowboy from 1917 to 1923. He became a western star in his own right during the Twenties, but was unable to continue in heroic parts with the advent of sound, due to the unsuitability of his voice. Instead, he turned his attention to playing villains in "B" feature westerns and serials of the Thirties, and organizing stunts for these and other films. He also became highly aware of the vital importance of creating equipment to make stunting safer.

The wagon stunt

To overturn a speeding wagon, stuntmen had until this time relied on the primitive methods of digging up the ground and running the wheels into holes or building up rocks in the hope of hitting them and so upsetting the speeding vehicle. Canutt experimented with lengths of airplane cable attached under the front axle of the wagon, with the other end staked into the ground. The horse team then pulled the wagon past its measured point and it would somersault forward spectacularly. The horses were saved from injury by a carefully placed release mechanism that freed the horses from the speeding vehicle. One of his toughest assignments, however, was to leap a wagon and pair off a cliff with four men aboard in **Dark Command** (1940). He managed this by running a team and wagon down a chute, enabling it to build up momentum. There was a special cable attached from the back of the wagon to the cliff top to prevent the vehicle from crashing down on the occupants. The wire was hidden from view by an exploding can of

"Yakima" Canutt was probably the greatest stuntman of all time, being awarded a special Oscar at the Academy Awards ceremony in April 1967. Here and overleaf he is seen showing his full range of skills.

Top left:
Canutt executes a "running W" fall in **Stagecoach** (1939). This kind of stunt has since been outlawed since it was extremely dangerous and could easily result in the horse's death. The stunt involved tying one end of a length of wire to a fixed object and the other end to the horse's forelegs, and then riding him beyond the

maximum length of the wire, so pulling the legs from under him making horse and rider tumble to the ground.

Above:
Canutt performs a tricky horse-to-coach transfer, using a specially designed "L" stirrup to ensure his foot does not get caught.

dust and bits of broken wood.

Canutt also broke new ground in staging bar-room brawls. In the early days, stuntmen used to allow the leading actors to punch them about the upper body and shoulders, but drew the line at taking one in the face. Working to the tight schedules of a Monogram western or a Mascot serial where an in-demand stuntman might be taking part in four fist fights a week, such punishment could be quite damaging. With the advent of sound, Canutt realized that it would be possible to overcome this problem using strategically placed cameras. First, punches were thrown deliberately intending to miss the opponent's face by inches; second, the opponent snapped his head sideways at the right moment, looking as if he had just been thumped by a fierce right hook; third, a sound effect of flesh hitting bone would be added to complete the illusion.

As a stuntman, Canutt's career lasted 15 years – 10 years longer than the average working life of a stuntman in those days – but during that time he had amassed a staggering 150 credits, which works out at an average of 10 films a year. Among these were: **Stagecoach** (1939), **Gone With The Wind** (1939),

Jesse James (1939), **They Died With Their Boots On** (1940) and **Gentleman Jim** (1942). He had doubled nearly every major star who ever rode a horse, including John Wayne, Clark Gable, Henry Fonda and Roy Rogers.

In 1941 he suffered his last, and worst injury when he broke both ankles leaping from the top of a speeding stagecoach into a concealed net.

Canutt decided to retire as far as active stunting was concerned. But his career in films was far from finished. Within five years he was established as a second unit director and for the next 30 years devised and directed the action sequences for some of Hollywood's more successful box-office hits. They included the jousting scenes in **Ivanhoe** (1953), the chariot race in **Ben Hur** (1959), the gladiatorial combats in **Spartacus** (1960), and the massed armies at the siege of Valencia in **El Cid** (1961); the comedy riding scenes in **Cat Ballou** (1965), the desert warfare in **Khartoum** (1966), the fight on the cable car in **Where Eagles Dare** (1967) and the blinding of the horses in **Equus** (1976). His innovations have become the blueprint for all the modern devices employed by present day stuntmen.

Left:
Canutt takes a dramatic fall
in **Virginia City** (1940), by
riding his horse into a small
concealed pit, making both
crash to the ground in front
of the lens.

Right:
Canutt, to the right of the
picture, leaps to safety from
an exploding wagon.

ELIMINATING THE "X" FACTOR

Stunting is not a profession for daredevils. The overriding task that confronts the modern stuntman when tackling a new stunt is calculating the danger and eliminating the risks.

But no matter how studiously a stunt is worked out in advance, there is always the possibility of an unforeseen danger. In the film world, this is known as the "X" factor.

Harvey Parry claimed that the worst injury he ever suffered was a broken back resulting from a three-foot fall from a wooden sidewalk. This occurred during the making of **North to Alaska** (1960) when, as a drunk, he had to slip on a sidewalk and fall into the road which was covered in snow. The "X" factor was, in this instance, a two-inch peg sticking out of the road but hidden by the snow. Parry landed right on top of it.

Another unfortunate stuntman was A.J. Bakunas, who had set a record 234-feet high fall in making **Hooper** (1978). For **Steel** (1979), he attempted to break his own record by jumping from 315 feet into an airbag designed by himself. In full view of 1,000 horrified onlookers in Lexington, Kentucky, he plunged from the top of an unfinished tower block.

On impact, the airbag split and in spite of the safety layer of cardboard cartons mounted on sprung planking, he crashed into the asphalt roadway and died 15 hours later of multiple internal injuries. No one is quite sure why it happened. Probably the answer lies in the "X" factor. A falling body passes through the air at something like 72 feet per second, reaching a terminal speed of 133 miles per hour. At this speed the body weight is increased disproportionately. Therefore the death of this unfortunate stuntman can only be ascribed to his weight exceeding the safety regulations which the airbag was designed to take.

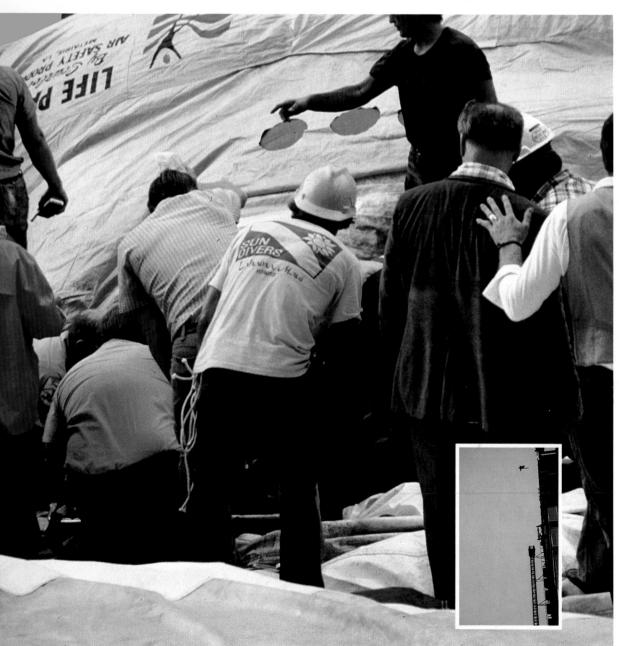

This page:
The death of high-fall specialist A.J. Bakunas during the filming of **Steel** (1979). Bakunas, who held the record for the highest fall on film at that time – 234 feet from a helicopter in **Hooper** (1978) – was killed when he attempted to eclipse his own record by pitching himself from a 315-feet high office block in Lexington, Kentucky; the air-bag, his own design, split and failed to cushion his fall.

Right:
A spectacular shot from **The Stunt Man** (1980), in which a Vietnam veteran poses as a stunt man for a sinister film director while escaping from the police.

MODERN APPROACHES TO STUNTING

Most stuntmen will agree that the four most risky stunts are high falls, fire, motorcycle crashes and work with horses, though not necessarily in that order. Let's take a look at how the modern stuntman goes about setting them up.

The high fall

Over the past 20 years the advances made in the design of equipment to assist the safety of the high falling stuntman have been so enormous that records are being shattered constantly. From the 60-foot maximum fall of 25 years ago the modern stuntman has gone to 285 feet freefalling to 800 feet with a con-cealed parachute, to over 1,000 feet on a wire assisted tumble. All of this is a far cry from the falls into nets and mattresses of the Silent days. Cardboard cartons covered with a layer of mattresses were the standard safety device for high falls for the best part of 50 years. The rule of thumb was one layer of boxes for every 10 feet that the stuntman had to fall. For any fall over 30 feet it was advisable to put a layer of flattened cartons between the layers of boxes. The bottom layer of boxes were roped together to prevent them blowing outwards on impact, so causing the entire rig to collapse. The method usually worked, but only in so far as it catered for falls of less than 60 feet. But, with a cost of $2.50 per carton, the safety rig was beginning to become more expensive than the stunt-man.

The crash pad

In the mid-Sixties the crash pad appeared. This was a canvas rectangle that could be filled with foam rubber and covered with a tarpaulin. It was used as an aid for such sporting events as the high-jump and pole-vaulting. The stuntmen adopted it for their own use in falls of up to 80 feet.

Next came the airbag, the credit for its development going to ex-circus performer Bob Yerkes. The airbag is most usually constructed of nylon, being 15 feet by 20 feet, and 6 feet high. This oversized mattress is inflated by an electric fan pumping warm air into it, and can be used for falls of over 100 feet. The design has now been refined to allow for a fall from almost any angle.

The wire assisted fall is a useful, if limited, device. Adapted from the "descender", used in U.S. parachute training, it enables the stuntman to drop feet first from high buildings or over waterfalls. Its disadvantage is that it is too rigid a device to use for anything more ambitious.

The one danger common to all such safety devices is that they can breed feelings of overconfidence. When the stuntman starts to believe that he has mastered a routine just because he has done a stunt a number of times without undue mishap then it is time for him to reassess all the dangers in order to avoid complacency.

Two ways to dive from a great height. *Above:* In Madrid, "Tap" Canutt demonstrates the safety of a "high fall rig" (with mattress-covered trampoline) to actor Stephen Boyd for **The Fall of the Roman Empire** (1964).

Below:
Setting up a "box rig" for a high fall in **Indiana Jones and the Temple of Doom** (1984). Cardboard cartons are stacked and then covered by mattresses. The rule of thumb is a layer of boxes for every 10 feet.

Fire

Very few people actually burn to death. Most deaths by fire can be attributed to asphyxia, in other words the victims suffocate before the flames engulf their bodies. Cold comfort to the victim, of course, but heartening to a stuntman about to set himself on fire, or so you might think. For holding one's breath can lead to hypothermia, pneumonia or even brain damage. Shock is another potential danger. So, too, is the possibility of third-degree burns.

The stuntman has to wear protective clothing to survive. Next to his skin he wears a pair of "long johns" that have been treated with a flame proofing agent. Over this is placed a racing driver's "silver suit" which is aluminum based to prevent the flesh from blistering. Next he'll put on an outer garment such as a pair of overalls made of a flame-resistant material. On his head he wears a racing driver's mask, not unlike a ski mask, and over that a flame-proof mask shaped in the features of a human head and face — often taken from a life mask of the actor for whom he's doubling. Next come flame-resistant gloves and boots. To overcome the problem of oxygen starvation he will have a cylinder of bottled air fitted under his arm, with a tube leading to his mouth.

When it comes to the fire sequence he is covered with an inflammable paste mixture which gives off a dramatically bright but not searing flame. Even so, he must limit the time he is alight. This is known as the "safety margin". Most stuntmen will allow themselves only a 20-second maximum safety margin, at which point the fire extinguishers are switched on, even if the scene has *not* been finished.

In the event of something going wrong while the shot is in progress, the stuntman will indicate by a pre-arranged signal — usually by lying spreadeagled on the floor — that he is in trouble and the flames must be extinguished immediately. This is the one time when the stunt team and the special effects crew can overrule the director on a movie set. Surprisingly, most stuntmen will prefer to have fellow stunters standing by with the extinguishing equipment. Too many people, even firemen, tend to stand transfixed at the sight of a pre-meditated self-immolation. Also, flames surrounding the stuntman can suddenly leap 12 feet in the air which prompts the inexperienced fire fighter to stand so far back that he would be too late in coming forward in an emergency.

The three shots from **The Towering Inferno** (1974) show actress Susan Flannery trapped in a burning room in the upper stories of the tallest building in the world. As the flames engulf her, she throws a chair through the window to try and escape the fire. Instead, the rush of air to the outside sucks her, burning, to her death on the sidewalk hundreds of feet below. A male stunt double (probably Dick Johnson) took the flaming dive for her, wearing asbestos gloves.

Explosions

For the stuntman the dangers in being blown through the air by an explosion are not from the explosive device itself, which is controlled, but from the method used to propel him and from the lack of an adequate area of padding on which he can safely land.

There are a number of propelling devices that can be used depending on the type of explosion required, and whether the stuntman is to be thrown forwards or backwards.

For instance if a small bomb or hand grenade is the motivating power, then a small trampoline capable of pitching him 8 to 10 feet through the air will be used. For a stunt like this, where the impact with the ground will not be much harder than a fall from a cantering horse, it is possible to use the same safety technique, digging up the falling area and filling it with sand or moss peat. If the explosion is larger, requiring the stuntman to be blown higher, a full-sized trampoline will be used, often concealed in a pit. The stuntman then stands on a ladder off-camera and drops down onto the trampoline. As his feet make contact with the trampoline's surface the cameras roll, and the special effects man will ignite the explosive charge, usually placed in a large pot between the camera and the trampoline. When the charge, which is covered with cork, peat, dust and pieces of styrofoam detonates, it obscures the stuntman for a fraction of a second before he somersaults through the air and lands on a hidden crash pad.

Left:
A dramatic example of a complete immolation fire stunt. The stuntman's head is protected by a flame-proof mask while the burning agent (probably petroleum jelly) has been spread over his back and legs only. Note that he is being filmed against a dark background to help make the flames look even fiercer.

Below:
British and Dutch stuntmen collaborated to create the realistic battle scenes for **A Bridge Too Far** (1977).

The air-ram

If the stuntman is required to fly backwards from the explosion an "air-ram" is sometimes used. This piece of equipment is a hinged board with a strong spring in the center, doubled over and held by a catch, which is attached to an oxygen cylinder. The stuntman stands on the board and on the cue: "Action!" a jet of compressed air releases the catch and throws the stuntman from 5 to 15 feet into the air. However, it is not without its drawbacks.

During the making of **1941** (1979) stuntman Gary Epper was thrown so hard by an air-ram that he missed his crash pad and fractured a collarbone. Another device for throwing stunt artists over long distances is the "teeterboard", a circus device involving a stuntman standing on one end while his partner leaps onto the other. A practical working knowledge of gymnastics or experience in the circus ring is essential.

Driving for safety

The sight of a crashing horse-drawn chariot or stagecoach and team, with all the accompanying flailing hooves and uprush of dust, or a car overturning to a shriek of brakes, grinding metal and shattering glass, will seem far more dangerous to the cinema audience than to the stuntman. Most vehicle crashes are, in fact, much easier to execute than you would think.

For an automobile crash, a "roll bar" – a piece of curved tubular scaffolding – is fitted behind the driver's seat above his head to prevent the car's roof caving in and crushing him. All internal fixtures such as door handles and ash trays, are removed since they can cause serious injuries. The driver is padded on the elbows, shins, knees and back, and wears a surgical collar as protection against a "whiplash" to the neck. Finally, the driver wears a crash helmet and straps himself in with a full safety harness. To avoid fires or explosions, the car is filled with the precise amount of fuel required, and no more. All excess oil is removed.

A six car pile-up in the movie directed by ex-stuntman Hal Needham, **Smokey and the Bandit II** (1980). The film starred Burt Reynolds, Jackie Gleason and Sally Field.

Below:
French stunt driver Remy Julienne smashes into a horizontal barrier, taking the top off his car in **A View to a Kill** (1985). This tricky stunt had to be performed at 60 mph in order to get maximum pressure to break off the car's roof.

Right:
The Man with the Golden Gun (1974), the ninth film in the James Bond series, the first film to have a computerized stunt. This was worked out on an apparatus at Cornell University by W.J. Milligan Jr. – although the stunt itself was performed by Bumps Willard. The result was the famous "spiral jump", in which James Bond (Roger Moore) in an AMC Hornet drives up a ramp which has been disguised as a broken bridge over a canal, turns over and lands on the far bank right side up.

Overleaf:
The closing shot of **Vanishing Point** (1971), in which the hero (Barry Newman) is killed in a head-on collision with two bulldozers. Credit for this and the many pile-ups in the film goes jointly to Cary Loftin and Louis Elias.

Left:
David Soul, playing a villainous police cadet, is doubled by Dan Robinson on an out-of-control police motorcycle which plunges 45 feet into San Francisco harbor in the final reel of **Magnum Force** (1974). A wide-angle lens on the camera made the drop appear to be twice as great.

Right:
Motorcycle specialist Mike Runyard doubles for Sean Connery during this leap over a fast-moving car in **Never Say Never Again** (1983).

Motorcycle crashes

Very few car stunts are executed at more than 50 miles per hour. Since the driver is hardly visible, it is possible to speed up the action by means of running the camera at very fast frame speeds to simulate a car traveling at up to 60 or 90 miles per hour.

Very few of these rules, however, can be applied to the motorcycle smash. Apart from racing leathers and possibly a crash helmet, the motorcycle stuntman has almost no safety cover to rely on. Also, because the crash will certainly involve the rider and bike parting company, the process of speeding up the film on camera can only be minimal in case the natural human reactions look as if they belong to a Charlie Chaplin comedy.

The least risky crash appears to be the "racing broadside", which is achieved by suddenly twisting the handlebars to the right or left, so putting the bike into a side skid and "laying it flat". However, this presents the problem of hitting a concrete roadway at anything from 25 to 40 miles an hour, crushing either leg, depending on the weight of the bike being used, and scraping the flesh off either legs, buttocks, ribs and underarms or elbows.

Another method of crashing involves the stuntman throwing himself off the bike while going into a skid, kicking the bike away and sliding after it. But there is always the danger of catching a limb or piece of clothing on part of the machine and being dragged along by the bike. Going headfirst over the handle-bars presents the rider with the possibility of the motorbike running over him. To offset the hazards of this particular danger, a new device has been created involving a wire attached at one end to the pillion of the bike, and at the other to a fixed object, so preventing it from careering on over the rider. This technique was shown to great effect by Buddy Joe Hooker in **Hooper**. However, the greatest series of motorcycle stunts was in the film **Electra Glide in Blue** (1973).

Below:
Buddy Joe Hooker performs a spectacular motorbike tumble while doubling for Burt Reynolds in **Hooper**, the 1978 film about stuntmen.

Far right:
Hearts of the West (1975). The second part of a stunt, involving a 12-foot leap onto the back of a waiting horse, that the film's insurers would not allow star Jeff Bridges to perform lest he injured himself.

Horses

Most stuntmen agree that working with horses is the most dangerous form of stunting there is, since they are unpredictable animals with a frightening turn of speed. They can also be extremely obstinate, and will only perform stunts or tricks when they want to do so. They can *not* be bullied. Despite these reservations, horses have presented stuntmen with their widest range of action stunts and movie goers with their largest selection of thrills.

There are basically three different ways of falling off a horse: you can take a backfall as it rears up; a saddle fall to the left or right when cantering; and fly head-first over its shoulder by getting him to pull up sharply, as if he's refusing a jump. Each of these falls requires the application of the "L" stirrup, invented by "Yakima" Canutt to replace the normal riding stirrup, and adjusted to a slightly shorter length. This stirrup enables the rider to thrust himself well clear of the horse when he comes to take his fall.

Other devices which enable the stunt rider to achieve a spectacular fall are the *somersault harness*, *jerk harness* and *dragging rig*. The first is a tight leather vest with a hook set between the shoulder blades. A short length of wire with a ring at either end is slipped over the hook in the back of the jacket and attached to another hook at the back of the saddle. It must be so tight that the stuntman is pulling against it. With his "L" stirrups hitched well up, the rider puts his horse into a canter and as he passes over the prepared ground, pushes himself backward toward the horse's rump. The wire helps to guide him over in a backward somersault, unhooking itself en-route.

The same jacket can be adapted for use as a jerk harness. The hook between the shoulder blades is removed and a length of airplane wire substituted. A second stuntman, holding a rifle or spear, stands at the place where the rider will fall off. When the rider canters up to the spot, the spear holder steps to one side and swings the weapon at him, but making minimum contact. However, it seems to the audience that the rider has been dealt a powerful blow since the wire, now at full stretch, has hauled him suddenly backwards off the horse.

The dragging rig is used to give audiences the impression that the horseman has fallen from the saddle, leaving his foot caught in the stirrup. A foot leather strap is attached firmly to the stirrup, threaded up the stuntman's trouser leg and is either held by him or attached to his leather jerkin on a quick release mechanism. Consequently, there is no strain on the rider's leg and he can release himself whenever there is a danger of the runaway horse trampling or kicking him.

A fine example of horse training can be seen in **The Long Riders** (1980), in which horse and rider are seen to leap through a plate glass window. The glass of course was not glass at all but "santalite", a brittle, resin-based clear plastic. To complete this stunt, the horse is trained first to jump through an empty wooden frame, approximately the size of the window through which he will leap before the camera. Then he is urged to jump through the frame with balsa wood cross-pieces. Next tissue paper is taped into the

Right:
The start of the famous chase scene in **Raiders of the Lost Ark** (1981). Terry Leonard, doubling for Harrison Ford, makes a transfer from a galloping horse to the speeding truck containing the Lost Ark. A quarter horse (a saddle horse capable of high speed over short distances) at full gallop is running at almost 30mph.

Below:
An exciting example of a trained falling horse in action. This shot is from **The Magnificent Seven** (1960).

cross-pieces and again the horse jumps through the window. Finally, heavy celluloid is substituted. The purpose of all these stages is to build up the horse's confidence for the final jump, although he may be somewhat taken aback by the noise the santalite makes, which is almost as loud as the sound of shattering glass.

Horse falls

It is a rule of all U.S.-based films that any falling horse must be made to fall "on the bit". Training a horse to fall in this way is perhaps the most difficult horse stunt there is because it goes so much against the animal's nature.

One of the methods involves tying up the horse's left foreleg, then pulling its head around to the right, so causing it to lie down on its side. This is an age-old veterinary technique used to examine mares who are in foal.

Naturally, horse falling can only be done on a "falling bed" – ground that has been dug up, turned over with sand or moss peat set evenly into it. This is essential since the typical horse used for this kind of work weighs around half a ton and can easily injure itself.

Of course, not all horses can be turned into stunt horses. It takes a certain build and a lot of boldness, which the average horse does not possess. But with the right choice of animal and a lot of patience, horses can be made to fall, rear, ride through fire and explosions, up a flight of stairs onto a balcony, jump through windows and even leap off cliffs.

Vital support

Although the stunt artist is usually the star of any action scene, it would be wrong to suggest that it is by

Below:
A tricky fall from a horse which the stuntman, disguised as a Red Indian, has to perform without the aid of saddle or stirrups. Unless he times it correctly he could easily slide under the horse's belly and be trampled on by its back legs.

Famous son of a famous father, "Tap" Canutt, son of "Yakima" Canutt, demonstrates the technique of training a horse to fall "on the bit" (*above left*). First, with the aid of a lunging rein, the horse's head is turned, causing him to lose his balance and lie down on his side. Later (*below left*) he does it at a canter. Note the ground is well broken up and filled in with sand.

Below:
Joe Canutt sustained a cut on his chin which required eight stitches, and suffered delayed shock and concussion following this sensational feat for the climax of the famous chariot race sequence in **Ben Hur** (1959).

his efforts alone that the hazardous sequences in a film script become realities on the screen. Any spectacular film stunt is almost certainly the result of the combined talents of artistic and technical personnel working together as a team.

At the top of the list is the producer, who in the case of a big spectacular film must be sufficiently experienced to budget for all the necessary effects. This includes hiring a director who can handle such scenes; if they are beyond him then a second unit director is usually taken on.

The first second unit director of any note was B. Reeves Eason, a former cowboy, circus performer and stuntman who, in order to get some added thrills out of the silent version of the chariot race in **Ben Hur** (1926), is reputed to have offered the then extravagant total fee of $300 to the first three drivers across the finishing line.

Such enterprise so impressed the powers in charge of the Hollywood film studios that, for the next quarter of a century, "Breezy", as he was known, was the first choice to direct such action scenes. His best work includes the charge of the British cavalry in **The Charge of the Light Brigade** (1936), the jousting sequences for **The Adventures of Robin Hood** (1938), the burning of Atlanta in **Gone With the Wind** (1939) and the World War One trench battles for **Sergeant York** (1940).

"Breezy" set about his work in a very different way to a documentary film maker filming a real battle. Contemporary audiences required more blood and action than was usually found in newsreels of real catastrophes, which were often tame in comparison. The best way of capturing such excitement was not by showing a general melee but by concentrating on a few dramatic details.

Left:
Jan-Michael Vincent, cast as a stuntman in **Hooper** (1978), is dragged behind a runaway chariot. The actor is assisted in this stunt by a miniature ski strapped to his chest to facilitate a smoother run over the broken terrain.

Right:
Sean Connery leaps from an exploding building during the making of **Never Say Never Again** (1983).

Below:
Actors Christopher Walken and Robert De Niro hang precariously from the skids of a helicopter during the escape scene in **The Deer Hunter** (1979). Concealed safety harnesses and wires attached to the main structure of the aircraft were almost certainly used to ensure their safety.

Second unit director

It is the job of the second unit director to expand the often skeletal descriptions of scenes of action written by the film's scriptwriter, which on occasion can be as brief as "– a fight ensues". From this instruction, a detailed shot list describing every movement made by each of the characters in the sequence must be assembled. Eason's scripting of the escape of Rhett Butler and Scarlett O'Hara through the backstreets of the burning city of Atlanta in **Gone With the Wind** ran to eight pages. His description of the train wreck in **Duel in the Sun** (1947) ran from one page in the original screen writer's treatment to 15 pages in the final shooting script.

Once the second unit director is given his budget he is in complete charge of the shooting of the scenes that he has been engaged to direct, with his own cameraman and crew. The stunt co-ordinator is the only person who can overrule him, usually only in the interest of safety.

"Yakima" Canutt worked in both jobs in his time,

and is aware of the problems involved. As stunt co-ordinator in charge of the chariot race for the re-make of **Ben Hur** (1959), he encountered a lack of co-operation from the film's production manager, Henry Henixson.

Usurping completely Canutt's authority as the stunt co-ordinator, Henixson announced that he had already made arrangements to film the chariot race in Italy, using Italian stuntmen. Canutt disagreed, wanting to hire experienced men from Hollywood. Henixson's response was to ignore him and turn his hearing aid down. In desperation, Canutt took his objections to the higher authority of Ed Mannix, MGM's studio manager, who gave him a sympathetic hearing and ordered that some of his demands be implemented.

As things turned out, the race was *the* major success of the film, which won no less than 11 Oscars at the 1959 Academy Awards ceremony. It is to the discredit of those unenlightened times that no prize was forthcoming for Canutt's work on the film.

Right:
Burt Reynolds performs his own stunt in a chase sequence in **Shamus** (1972). Contrary to popular belief, Reynolds was never a stuntman as such, rather an athletic actor. However, he was badly injured in a later scene which took him out of production for 12 days.

Below:
Burt Reynolds and friends in danger of capsizing on the Chattooga River in **Deliverance** (1972). Director John Boorman insisted on all the actors in the film doing the majority of their own stunts. Reynolds later described it as "the toughest picture I ever worked on".

Stunt man Martin Grace shows Harrison Ford, the star of **Raiders of the Lost Ark** (1981), how to go about evading just about everything that director Steven Spielberg could throw at him in this thrilling escape scene. In the filmed sequence, Ford performed all the action himself under Grace's supervision.

Far left:
Jeff Bridges, playing a cowboy extra in **Hearts of the West** (1975), leaps through a ''santalite'' window with breakaway balsa wood supports. Although he performed this part of the stunt himself, the latter part, a drop from a balcony onto a horse's back, was considered to be too dangerous for the star to attempt.

This page:
The Godfather (1972). Marlon Brando as Mafia boss Don Vito Corleone is gunned down in a New York street. The 48-year-old superstar, playing a man 25 years his senior, achieved the effect of slower reflexes by having 10-pound weights attached to his shoes, plus copious body padding.

Overleaf:
A helicopter attack in Vietnam from **Apocalypse Now** (1979), shot in the Philippines and employing the specialist skills of pilots and explosives experts.

101

El Cid

A couple of years later Canutt encountered difficulties again, this time as second unit director on **El Cid** (1961), when the director, Anthony Mann, refused to allow him a free hand in the staging of the action sequences. Shooting the battle from a bridge 12 feet up, Mann got an excellent view showing the entire army moving against the defenders of the walls of Valencia. However, he demonstrated a marked lack of expertise by asking Canutt to organize a number of horse falls among the tightly packed actors and extras. In the opinion of the more experienced Canutt, this was not only dangerous, but a waste of money.

Needless to say, the horsefalls were completely lost to the cameras photographing them, as Canutt had predicted, and they had to re-shoot the stunts from a lower, closer angle. Later, Canutt had to take a firm stand over a mounted joust between El Cid and the villain, Don Martin. Once again, Mann interfered, but quickly realized that he couldn't win when faced with Canutt's greater experience.

After this episode, Canutt went on to create what is probably the most exciting reconstruction of a medieval trial by combat ever put on film. Using his two sons, Joe and Tap, to double for Charlton Heston and Christopher Rhodes respectively, he organized a combat scene which took less than half a paragraph to describe in the script, but nearly a week to shoot.

The special effects department had created a set of lances that would telescope three feet into the handle. The last third of the lance, leading up to the point, was made of balsa wood so that it would easily shatter on impact. These lances were placed in racks at either end of the field, so that as each successively shattered on contact with the opponent's shield, the riders could canter back to the lance rack before returning to the fray.

Using two cameras to film the scene, Joe and Tap were instructed by their father to charge each other three times, their lances breaking on each other's shields alternately. However, on the second charge, Tap's lance missed Joe's shield and caught him squarely in the chest, knocking the wind out of him. The next set-up on the schedule involved Joe taking a fall from the saddle, but in view of the last accident Canutt decided he should take a rest.

Day three saw Joe being knocked bodily from the back of his mount with the aid of a jerk harness and taking the saddle off at the same time. This was a planned set piece to be used to El Cid's advantage later in the scene. In knocking Joe from the saddle, Tap's lance shatters, so he draws a mace and charges at his opponent, flailing the weapon above his head. Joe defends himself with the only weapon he has, his

Part of the famous joust sequence featured in **El Cid** (1961) devised by "Yakima" Canutt. Charlton Heston and Christopher Rhodes try out their swordplay routine.

This shot from **A View to a Kill** (1985) shows that stuntmen have to master ways of avoiding fatal crashes as much as they do setting fire to themselves and getting involved in one hundred and one other horrific incidents.

shield – until it is knocked flying with a blow from the mace. Once again the special effects people aided this piece of action with wires on both the shield and Joe.

Tap turns his horse around and charges once more at the now unarmed Joe. Here Canutt's genius for the totally unexpected is demonstrated.

He has El Cid pick up his fallen saddle and, holding it in front of him, drop to his knees directly in the path of the oncoming horse and rider. There is a collision in which the two men and the horse somersault in a tangle of arms, legs, hooves and weapons. The scene was made possible by a combination of the expertise of five different departments – stunts, special effects, design, props and the cameraman who photographed it so brilliantly.

Achieving the impossible

This spectacular stunt was achieved by dressing up a dummy in El Cid's costume and setting it on the edge of a pit filled with cardboard boxes and covered over with a tarpaulin. This in turn was camouflaged with sand and dust. Tap Canutt then rode at full gallop towards the figure of El Cid. Just before he reached it, however, his mount stepped into the concealed pit, causing it to stumble and throw Tap clear over its head, while the horse's momentum carried it into the dummy figure, knocking it and the saddle flying.

After that there is a dazzling exhibition of sword-play, fought with both ordinary broadswords and large double-handers which brought both the film artists watching the fight to their feet and the movie audience in the theater to the edge of their seats with excitement. For this one sequence of magnificent action which lasts no longer than seven minutes in the finished film, a small army of people was required: the wranglers who supplied the horses; the armorers who supplied the swords and weapons; the wardrobe department who cleaned and repaired the costumes; the makeup artists who applied the lashings of blood; the props and stagehands who dug the pits and manhandled the mattresses and boxes. And, of course, not least the camera crew who captured it all on film, often taking as many chances as the stuntmen themselves – all these people and many more are essential to the filming of any big scene of action. But it was the genius of "Yakima" Canutt that brought them all together to create action on such a breathtaking and believable scale.

Below:
Actor Harrison Ford throws a mean right to the jaw of ex-wrestler Pat Roche. The blow misses by inches. Clever camera angles make it look as if it connects.

Right:
Terry Leonard performs the climactic stunt in the most exciting action sequence in **Raiders of the Lost Ark** (1981).

MAKEUP MAGIC

The art of movie makeup has come closer to hi-tech in the last five years than it had progressed in the preceding 50. In fact, until John Chambers' revolutionary work on the **Planet of the Apes** films, film makeup was firmly entrenched in the theater tradition.

The first person to take makeup past the greasepaint and powder stage was the legendary Lon Chaney. Though Chaney died over 50 years ago, there can be few people in the western world who wouldn't recognize a portrait of Chaney as **The Phantom of the Opera** (1925), and for this and his other films, he created his own makeups. What made them so remarkable was his vivid visual imagination backed by extraordinary facial contortions. For example, to widen his nostrils for the Phantom role, he slipped wire hoops into his nose. And to create the strange, wide-eyed look of the vampire in **London After Midnight** (1927) he pushed wire monocles under his eyelids.

At the start of the Thirties, Universal were preparing a horror follow-up to their smash hit **Dracula** (1931), which had starred Bela Lugosi with a thin scraping of white greasepaint on his face but not a fang in sight. The new project was to be called **Frankenstein** and was to star the then unknown Boris Karloff. The makeup man assigned to turn Karloff into a walking corpse was Jack Pierce. Pierce had never done anything like this before – nor had anyone else – and so approached his task with "the confidence of ignorance". Pierce later revealed how he thought up the Frankenstein look: he had begun by researching into anatomy, ancient and modern burial customs, criminology, electrodynamics and surgery, and discovered that there are just six ways in which a skull can be cut. Since Dr. Frankenstein was not a surgeon he would obviously have opted for the simplest method, which is rather like taking a knife to cut off the top half of a boiled egg. Having placed the brain inside he would then replace the top part of the skull, clamping it down. "That's the reason," Pierce said, "that I decided to make the monster's head square and flat, like a box, and dig that big scar across the forehead and have metal clamps hold it together." Later, he attached a metal stud to either side of the neck as an electricity inlet since, in effect, the monster is a huge electrical gadget jerked into life by lightning.

However, the metal forehead clamps made an appearance only in early versions of the makeup. But there was still something not right. It was actor Karloff who spotted the flaw. "The monster was inarticulate," said Karloff. "When the audience first sees him

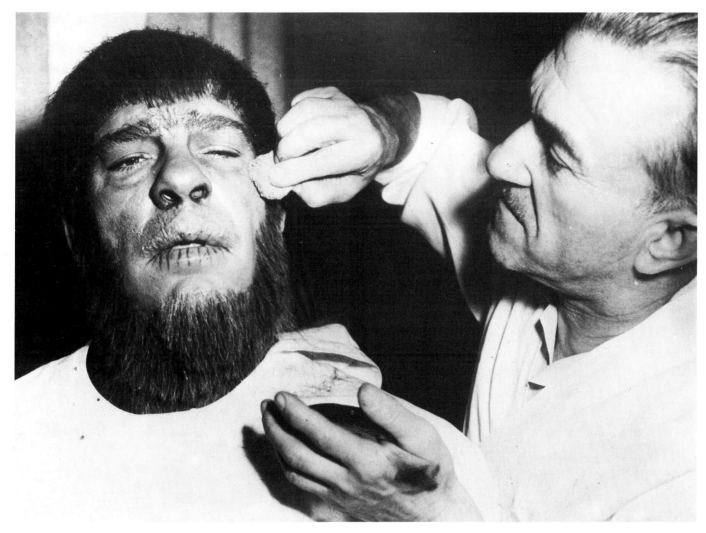

he is only five hours old. My first problem was not to let his eyes seem too intelligent, which is why I decided to use false eyelids which half veil the eyes."

Top horror

But what really made the makeup work was Karloff himself. The illusion was so designed that it left most of Karloff's expressive face free. The actor was allowed to act and "sell" the monster to the audience. Other actors have played the monster in the very same makeup yet not had the impact that Karloff did. Even so, Pierce became *the* special makeup man in Hollywood, turning out a very creditable string of

faces for Universal Studios. Pierce's talent kept Universal at the top of the horror heap throughout the Thirties and Forties, creating such unforgettable uglies as **The Mummy** (1932), with Karloff again; a makeup which remains memorable despite being seen for only a few seconds in the movie. Universal later revealed how the makeup effect was achieved. First, Karloff's dampened face was covered with cotton strips, which had been painted with spirit gum and collodion. Next, his ears were pinned back and an electrical dryer was used to create the facial wrinkles. Then his hair was bathed in clay and his whole body was wrapped in bandages. Apparently, by the end of

Right:
A rare close-up of Boris Karloff's makeup for his role in **The Mummy** (1932). The makeup was designed by Universal's makeup wizard Jack Pierce, and though only seen on the screen for a matter of seconds, the makeup remains one of the most memorable of the period.

Far right:
The most famous monster makeup of all: Boris Karloff as he appeared – under Jack Pierce's makeup – in **The Bride of Frankenstein** (1935). From the eyelids down, Karloff wears hardly any makeup at all, so allowing him complete freedom of expression. Most of the makeup is above the eyelids. The lids themselves are semicircles of rubber. The brow and forehead are also built up with rubber. For this film, the hairline has been singed back, a result of the fire at the end of an earlier film, **Frankenstein** (1931).

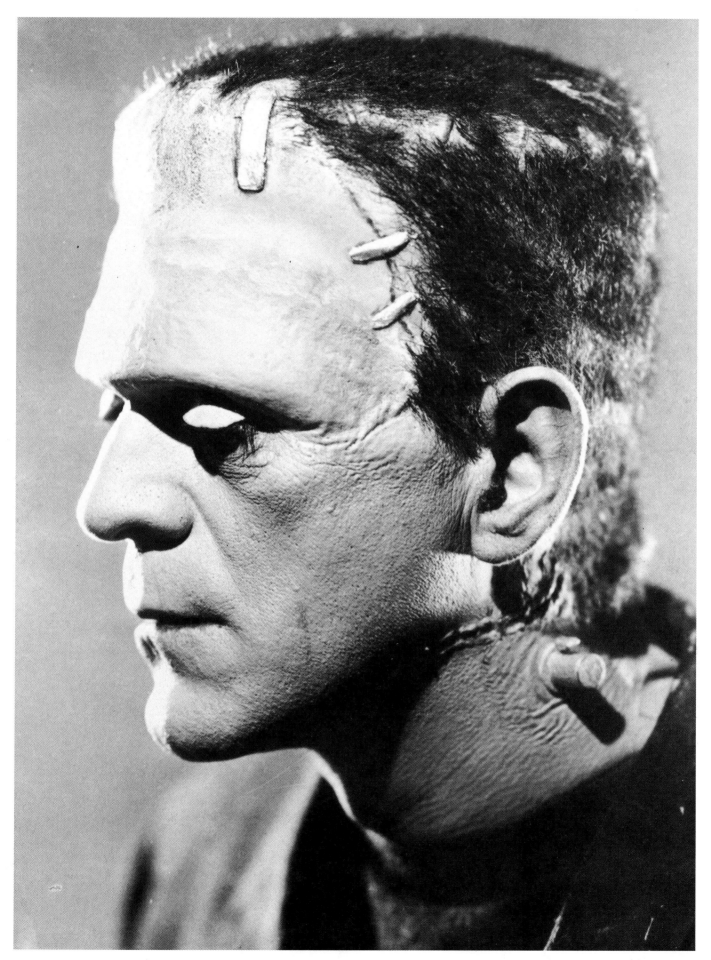

Right:
Jacqueline Pearce (*to the left*) as **The Reptile** (1966) – the creation of Hammer Films makeup man Roy Ashton. As is the case with all head masks, Ashton had to take a life cast of actress Jacqueline Pearce's head. But Pearce suffered from claustrophobia, making the casting of her head particularly difficult for Ashton. The final makeup remains one of Hammer's more interesting creations.

Far right:
Actor Lon Chaney Jr., son of the inventor of movie makeup, Lon Chaney Sr., as he appeared in the 1940 classic horror film **The Wolf Man**. Chaney's makeup here consisted of yak hair and greasepaint, a far cry from today's werewolf makeups, which seem to use more mechanics than face-fur.

this elaborate preparation Karloff couldn't move a muscle, let alone speak. Years later he said that his success was all down to the work of the makeup department. Of course he was exaggerating . . . but not that much!

By 1940, Karloff had graduated to more demanding roles than monsters, now played for Universal by new star Lon Chaney Jr. Though the son of the great horror actor was no great find as an actor, his name guaranteed brisk business at the box-office. Pierce was drafted in to create another winning makeup to shore up the flagging Universal horror cycle. Pierce went one better and gave audiences a makeup that

actually transformed on screen. It was an ambitious undertaking but Pierce pulled it off quite simply. He ensured that the plot required Chaney's character, Larry Talbot, to pass out, then had the camera cut to a close up of Chaney. He stopped the camera, and began applying makeup. By starting and stopping the camera he was able to build up the makeup on Chaney's face, and have the actor turn, literally before the audience's eyes, into **The Wolf Man** (1940). Forty years later, makeup wizard Rob Bottin used the same technique to have a man turn into a werewolf, this time even more gradually and graphically, in **The Howling**.

For the next 35 years movie makeup techniques did not advance much beyond the point where Pierce left it, except that blood became the rule not the exception. When Hammer Studios opened for business in the late Fifties, they took up where Universal, and Pierce, had left off, adding only a liberal splattering of Kensington Gore (the acting profession's term for stage blood) to liven up their technicolor productions. Hammer makeup man, Roy Ashton, revised some of the old Universal favorites like Frankenstein, Dracula, the Mummy and the Wolf Man and added a couple of his own. One of Ashton's creatures was **The Reptile** (1966), played by Jacqueline Pearce. To get the right effect Ashton had to undertake a lot of preliminary work. He studied living snakes and read about their anatomical arrangements before buying a large snakeskin from which he made a plaster cast. He then filled this with liquid plastic which, on hardening, gave a very precise replica. However Jacqueline Pearce found the headpiece something of a trial. She suffered from such dreadful claustrophobia that sometimes no sooner had she put it on than she had to tear it off!

The plaster cast of the actor's head was a major step forward from the Pierce days at Universal. In the Forties, actors had to sit for hours while the makeup artist applied the makeup straight on to the actor's face. But with the development of plastic prosthetics – foam rubber appliances cast in batches – elaborate makeups could be completed in far less time. The

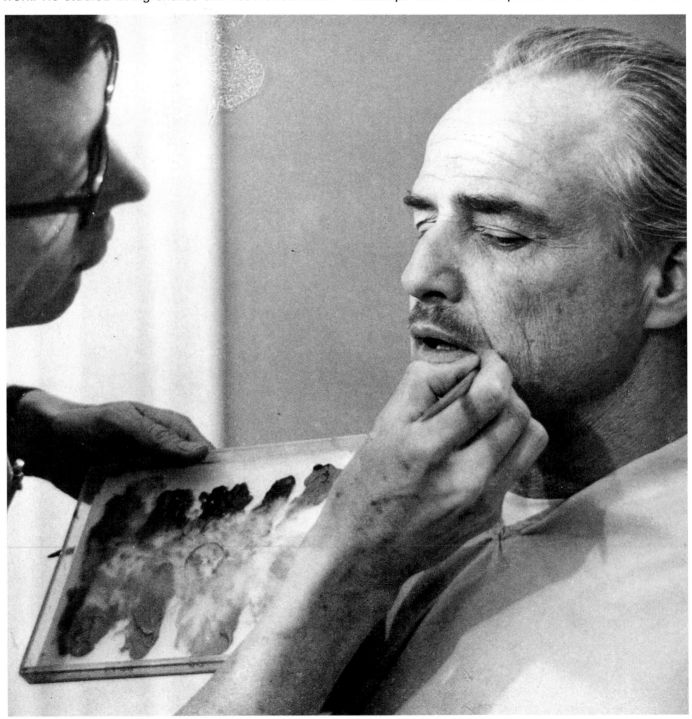

Below left:
Marlon Brando submits to the paintbrush of Dick Smith, the makeup man who aged him for his role in **the Godfather** (1972).

Below:
Makeup man Dick Smith has worked his magic on Brando for the closing reels of the film. Liquid latex is applied to the actor's face with a sponge in a kind of stippling fashion. The skin is then stretched and the latex is dried with a hair drier to produce this haunting look.

Right and far right:
Before and after: Dustin
Hoffman before the makeup
man Dick Smith got to work
on him and the aged
Hoffman under several
pounds of latex rubber for
Little Big Man (1970).

idea was that a cast was taken and a bust made. From there, the makeup man could sculpt an appliance directly onto the bust, then cast duplicates from this original. Consequently, the appliances could be attached with gum in minutes, instead of having to spend hours painstakingly building up the required image from mortician's wax.

Planet of the Apes

Appliances like these helped John Chambers create his award winning makeups for the **Planet of the Apes** films. Chambers explained in detail how these appliances were manufactured. Three were needed for each ape – one covering the forehead, one for the upper lip and one for the lower. Molds of each feature were made, drilled with holes and injected with foam rubber. It took six hours at a temperature of 200°F to set. However, none of these pieces could be used more than once since they tore when the makeup was removed. In 1968 Chambers won an honorary award

at the Oscars for his outstanding contribution to **Planet of the Apes** (1968).

The next major step forward in makeup technology was made during the filming of **The Exorcist** in 1973. The makeup man on that film was Dick Smith, who had aged Dustin Hoffman in **Little Big Man** (1970) and Marlon Brando in **The Godfather** (1972). Smith's innovation was to combine makeup with special effects, in effect bringing mechanization to his art. The most startling makeup effect in the whole movie is when Regan's (Linda Blair) head does a gut-wrenching 360° turn. This was achieved by taking a cast of Blair's *whole body* and then making a dummy. In the film it is the *dummy's* head that spins round, not Linda Blair's. A clever if macabre touch was the addition of radio controlled eyes to enhance the head's lifelike appearance.

But the effects that might seem the most compli-cated aren't always the most difficult ones to achieve. In Dick Smith's view Max Von Sydow's three-hour

Far right:
Tom Savini is the undisputed king of grisly horror makeup. In this scene from **Dawn of the Dead** (1979), a grotesque zombie threatens the heroes of the film – and the audience's stomach – with one deft stroke.

Right:
In this scene from **The Exorcist** (1973), Max von Sydow is actually wearing more makeup than the possessed girl (Linda Blair). When this film was made, von Sydow was 44, though he looked 74. That audiences didn't realise von Sydow was wearing makeup at all is a tribute to the skills of veteran makeup artist Dick Smith.

Right:
Young makeup innovator Tom Savini, who has worked on all the **Friday the 13th** series of horror films, created this simple but effective makeup trick for George Romero's vampire fable **Martin** (1978). The idea is that a razor blade is dragged along an actress's arm and blood flows from the resulting wound. How was it done? Using a blunt razor and a rubber bulb full of stage blood in the actor's hand. The blade moves across the skin and the stage blood trickles out of the bulb with the slightest pressure from the actor's fingers. . .

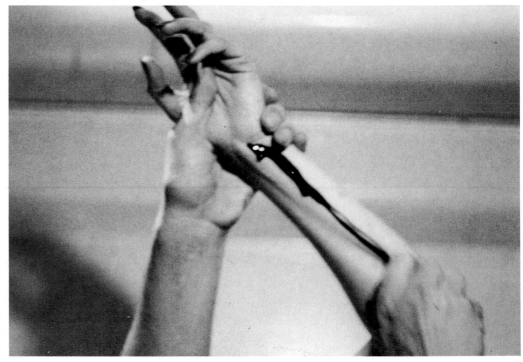

This sequence of photographs shows Christopher Tucker working on the famous makeup for **The Elephant Man** (1980). In the first picture (*left*), Tucker takes a cast of John Hurt's head. The second (*below*) shows Tucker at work, sculpting one of the foam rubber appliances that will be used to turn Hurt into the deformed John Merrick. Such appliances are sculpted on the cast of the actor's face. Then a cast is taken enabling the makeup team to cast duplicates as they're needed. The third picture (*overleaf*) shows the makeup as it finally appeared in the film.

(Pictures courtesy of Christopher Tucker.)

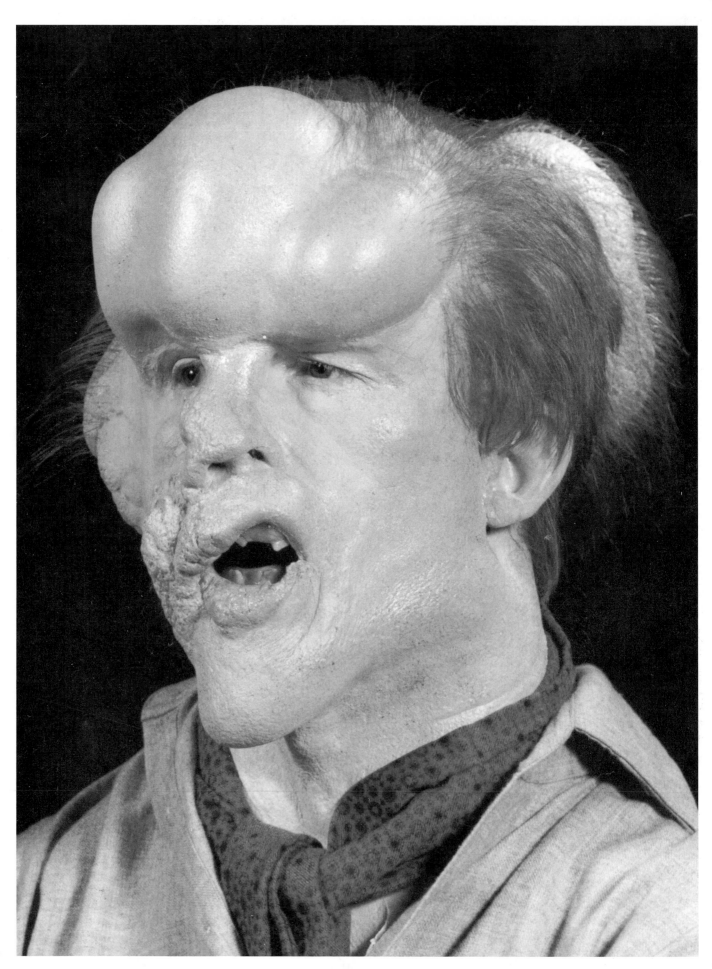

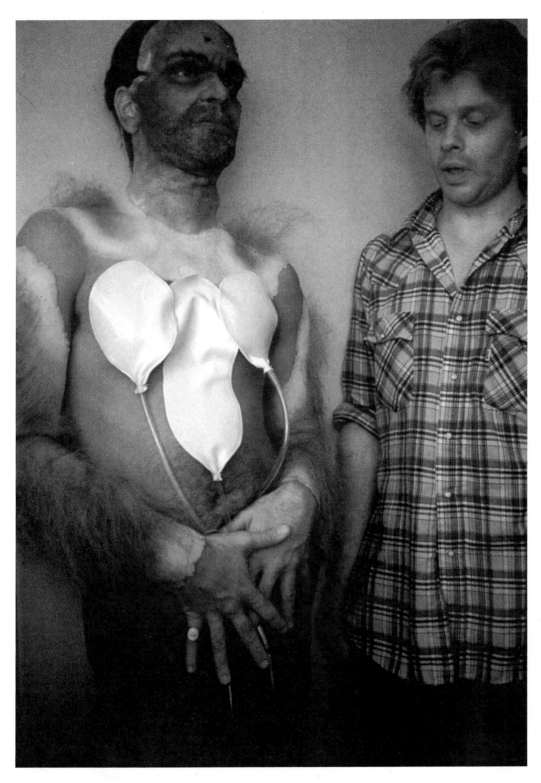

makeup in **The Exorcist** was more elaborate than Linda Blair's, and was only exceeded by Dustin Hoffman's makeup for **Little Big Man**. This was because director William Friedkin wanted some very detailed facial close-ups. The makeup department set about their work using pieces of foam latex, which were applied to his face, and heavy rubber mask greasepaint.

Smith had tried using this technique to age Marlon Brando in **The Godfather** but it proved too elaborate so they settled on liquid latex which, having been applied with a sponge to the face, stretched the skin and was then dried with a hairdrier. Blair also relied on similar appliances to those used in **The Exorcist** to apply to Brando's throat, chin, upper lip and sides of the head.

A few years later, Smith created another makeup first. In **The Fury** (1978) Smith dreamed up the pulsating veins which appeared on Andrew Stevens' forehead to signal that another psychic attack was coming. This was achieved by building inflatable channels into the foam plastic forehead appliance. The appliance was attached to Stevens' head and inflated for the cameras off-screen. This effect was later pick-

ed up and improved on by Rick Baker, who had assisted Smith on both **The Exorcist** and **The Fury**.

The same year, a makeup newcomer, Tom Savini, was hired by director George Romero to provide the gory illusions for a low budget vampire movie called **Martin**. In the opening of the movie, the title character, played by John Amplas, takes the arm of an unconscious girl and slices her arm from wrist to elbow with a blade. The wound seems to gush blood and the fingers twitch realistically, just in case anyone thinks it is a dummy arm. The scene is a show stopper and very, very simple, like all the best conjuring tricks. This ghastly effect was achieved by using a blunt razor blade and, concealed in the same hand, a baby

ear syringe filled with stage blood. As the blade was drawn along the skin the syringe was squeezed to release a line of blood. A couple of years later, Savini would be perpetrating more elaborate gore makeup effects for the notorious **Friday the 13th** series of films.

Master illusionist

Savini's shocking effects for **Friday the 13th** (1980) were clever enough, but they were ''sold'' to the audience by sophisticated editing. He wanted to trick audiences into believing that they were seeing a real ax crash into a woman's face, and relied on just five shots. First, a girl screaming; then the ax just missing

Far left:
Actor Robert Picardo is caught midway through a transformation in **The Howling** (1981). The effects for this film seemed all the scarier since they took place in dimly lit rooms.

Left and below:
Actor Robert Picardo under the makeup brush of Rob Bottin for his role in **The Howling** (1981). This particular makeup is for the scene in which Ricardo's character, Eddie Quist, has acid flung in his face, seconds before he begins to transform into a werewolf for the second time in the film. Bottin and his team first sculpt the holes in Picardo's face then lovingly add fake blood to complete the gruesome effect.

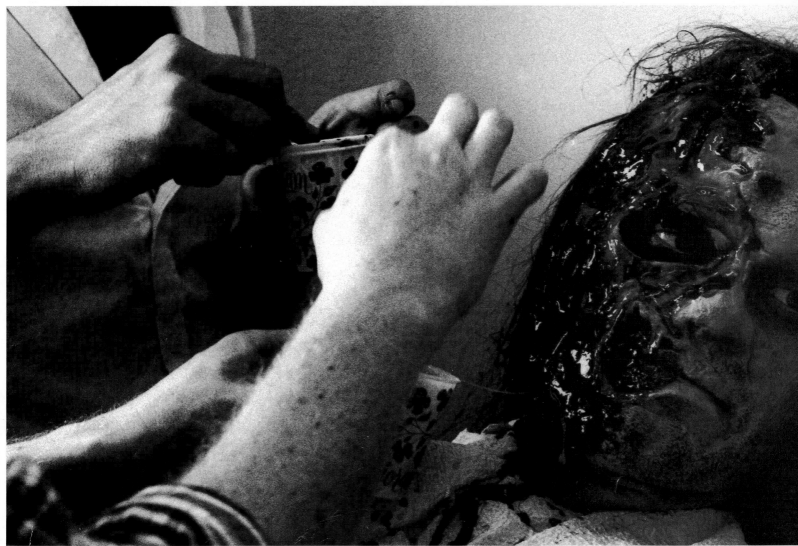

her head and splintering a window so that no one is in any doubt that it is real; the ax which now swings right at her (this time it's a foam rubber substitute); a real ax sticking out of the actress' false head; and finally a rubber ax glued to her real face. Seeing is believing, even if the action isn't always real.

While Savini was engineering it so that pretty American students could receive axes in their faces in **Friday the 13th**, British makeup man Christopher Tucker was using 15 foam latex appliances to convert

Previous page:
As a change from his usual zombies, director George A. Romero featured a Yeti in **Creepshow** (1982), a collection of tales in horror-comic style written by best-selling novelist Stephen King.

Left:
David Naughton keeps still as Rick Baker (out of view) pops a lens into place. This stage of the Oscar-winning makeup from **An American Werewolf in London** (1981) shows Naughton about halfway through his transformation to slavering werewolf. Though **American Werewolf** was beaten in the transforming wolf stakes by **The Howling** (1981), it was makeup man Rick Baker who invented the techniques and subsequently won the Oscar, the first ever awarded for movie makeup.

Below:
Rick Baker adds the finishing touches to the makeup for Griffin Dunne, who spends most of his time in **An American Werewolf in London** as one of the putrefying undead. The makeup on Dunne becomes progressively more horrifying.

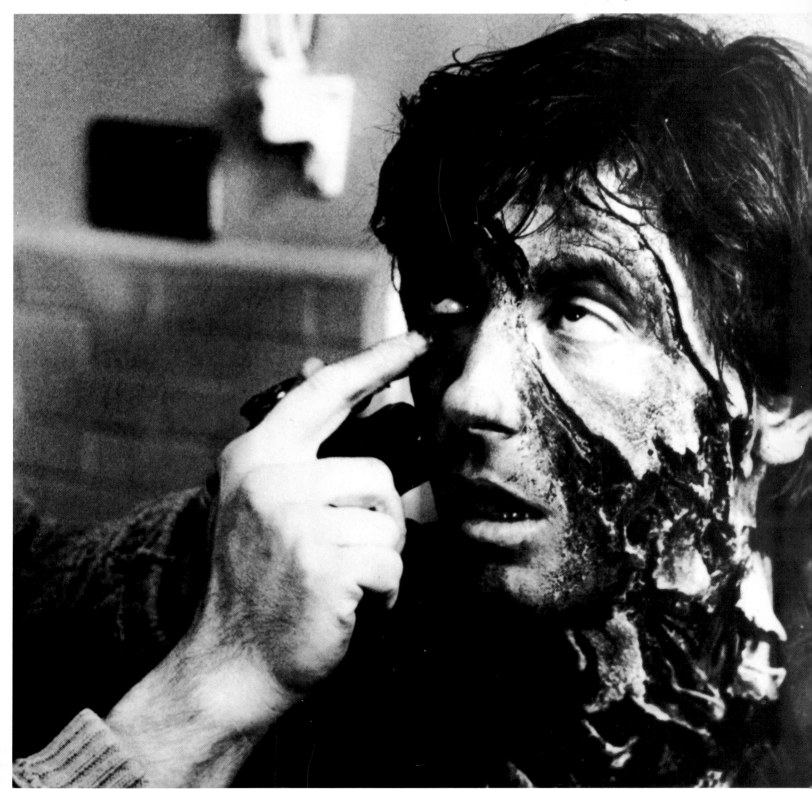

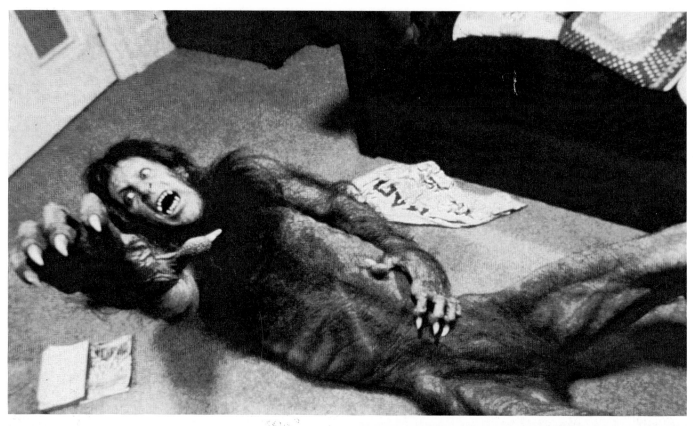

Far right:
A close-up of the hideous makeup created by Dick Smith for the exciting horror film **Ghost Story** (1981). Incredibly this picture actually shows a dummy, created over a life-sized cast of actress Alice Krige's head.

Above and right:
Though Rick Baker's makeup for **An American Werewolf in London** (1981) was some of the best ever created for the screen, winning the young technician an Oscar for his work, the suspense of this transformation scene was undercut by the bright, harsh lighting used by director John Landis. While this served to show Baker's makeup off to best advantage, it sacrificed the essential drama of the event, leaving too little to the audience's imagination.

The upper picture was filmed on a raised stage, so that the actor's body could be concealed below the floor while his head is attached to the dummy werewolf body. The lower picture shows the extendable hand-pieces which fitted over actor David Naughton's own hands.

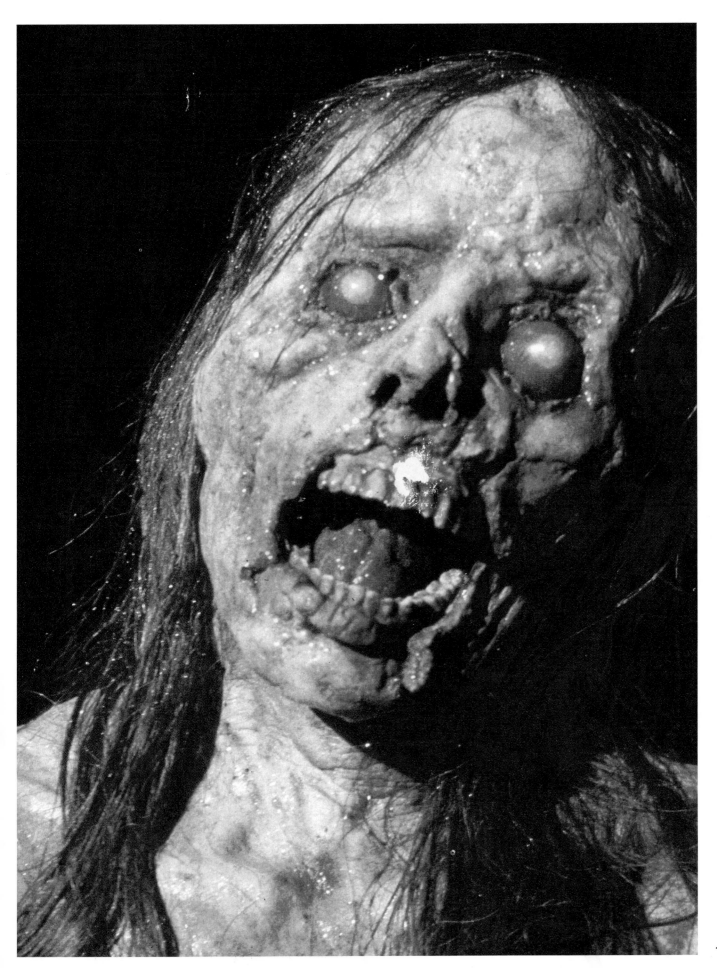

Above:
Veteran makeup man Dick Smith adds a couple of finishing touches to his dummy of actress Alice Krige for the horrifying finale of **Ghost Story** (1981). Behind Smith's ear you can make out the lens of the camera, lined up to shoot a horrifying close-up of the rotting corpse of the once-lovely young girl.

Far right:
Makeup magician Dick Smith poses in his Hollywood studio with a few of his creations, including William Hurt's mask from **Altered States** (1980), the 1970 **Little Big Man** mask, a fright mask from **The Sentinel** (1977) and a dummy head of Linda Blair from **The Exorcist** (1973).

Overleaf:
Makeup man Rob Bottin, wearing just a little makeup himself, poses with one of his extraordinary creations for **The Thing** (1982). The hair is real, but the teeth and eyes are not.

John Hurt into **The Elephant Man** (1980) in seven-hour long makeup sessions. Despite the grotesque appearance of Hurt in the film, Tucker is adamant that his was not a horror makeup. In fact quite the opposite. His sole intention was to create such deformity that his effects evoked pity, not terror.

Wolf men

The following year, horror movie fans in the audience for **The Howling** (1981) were in for something of a shock as makeup had taken an enormous leap forward in the hands of 20-year-old Rob Bottin. Using techniques taught to him by Dick Smith's one-time assistant Rick Baker, Bottin caused a man to transform into a wolf on screen. Not a werewolf, like Larry Talbot, but a huge, seven-foot wolf.

In the first stage of the transformation, actor Robert Picardo, who played the biggest, baddest werewolf in the movie, Eddie Quist, was fitted with a formidable set of teeth. Then latex appliances were glued to his face over rubber bladders. These bladders were inflated by off-camera assistants and made Picardo look as if his face were changing shape from the inside. From about this point, the actor bowed out and mechanical busts took over. In one stomach-churning shot, Picardo's (actually the dummy's) jawline seems to extend outward into a canine muzzle, accompanied by a series of bone-crunching sound effects. Finally, after what seems like hours, the transformation is

complete and the werewolf towers a good couple of feet over its screaming victim. The overall effect was very convincing, aided considerably by the gloomy, atmospheric lighting.

Not to be outdone, Rick Baker, who had invented many of the techniques used by Bottin in **The Howling**, gave movie audiences his own lycanthropic creation in **An American Werewolf in London** (1981). To improve on the Bottin transformation, Baker turned his actor, David Naughton, into a scary werewolf in a brightly lit room, and transformed not only his head,

Left and above:
This is the borderland where makeup and special effects meet. These extraordinary stills from John Carpenter's version of **The Thing** (1982) show part of the thing itself clinging to the ceiling. Naturally, what we see here is a dummy. The head has been sculpted from a life cast of the actor's face.

but his whole body too. Hollywood's Academy was so impressed that it created a special new makeup award to present to Baker.

Around the same time that Baker and Bottin were matching bladders trying to build a better werewolf, their mentor Dick Smith and his new assistant Craig Reardon were turning out some bladder-based makeups of their own for the Ken Russell movie, **Altered States** (1980). In one scene Dr Jessup (William Hurt) wakes up to find himself turning into a Mr. Hyde. He holds up his arm to see a changing shape, again managed with the help of the bladder-

under-the-appliance routine. What none of them knew at the time was that Joe Blasco, the makeup man on an early David Cronenberg-directed film **Shivers** (1974), had done it six years before. In a particularly horrific scene, Blasco had an actor's stomach bulge from within to simulate the movement of the obscene parasites featured in that film.

Dick Smith also created some particularly effective makeups for **Ghost Story** (1981), in which a group of elderly men are haunted by a murder they committed 60 years earlier. Alice Krige played the victim and avenger, along with a couple of repellent makeups

These pages and overleaf: Walt Disney's attempt at a more adult kind of film, **Something Wicked This Way Comes** (1983), called for an aging makeup to end all aging makeups. Bob Schiffer devised a process to enable actor Jonathan Pryce to age from about 35 to 135 on screen in full view of the audience. Pryce was aged with conventional makeup techniques for the first 50 years or so, by use of latex and foam rubber appliances. Later in the scene a dummy was substituted for the actor so that the aging could continue past death to the rotting corpse stage. Each makeup session with Schiffer and Pryce lasted about two and a half hours. "Nothing like it had ever been attempted before," said Schiffer later. "It was very tricky achieving the transition from a human head to a mechanical one. They had to match perfectly, with no margin for error."

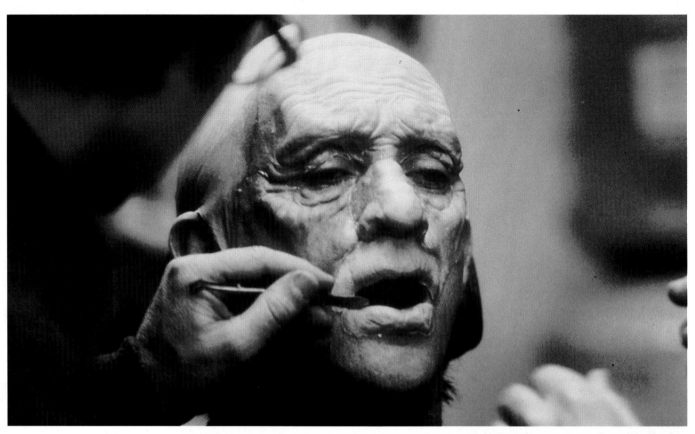

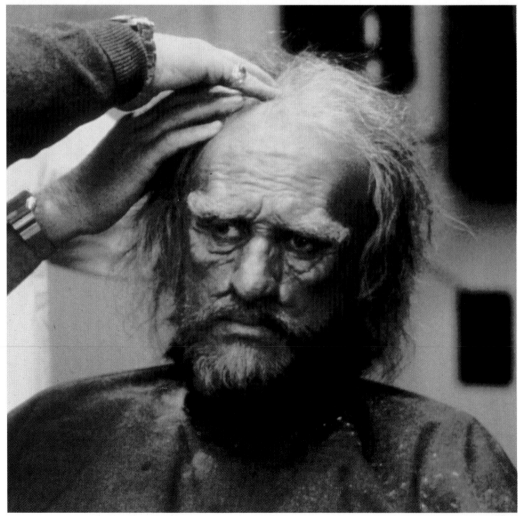

144

These pages:
The dramatic finishing touches are applied to Jonathan Pryce in **Something Wicked This Way Comes**.

Overleaf:
A drop of fake blood from Hammer's **Twins of Evil** (1971) – an easy day for the makeup man.

Overleaf right:
The robot gunslinger (Yul Brynner, parodying his **Magnificent Seven** image) reaches melting point in **Westworld** (1973), a makeup job also supplemented by a dummy.

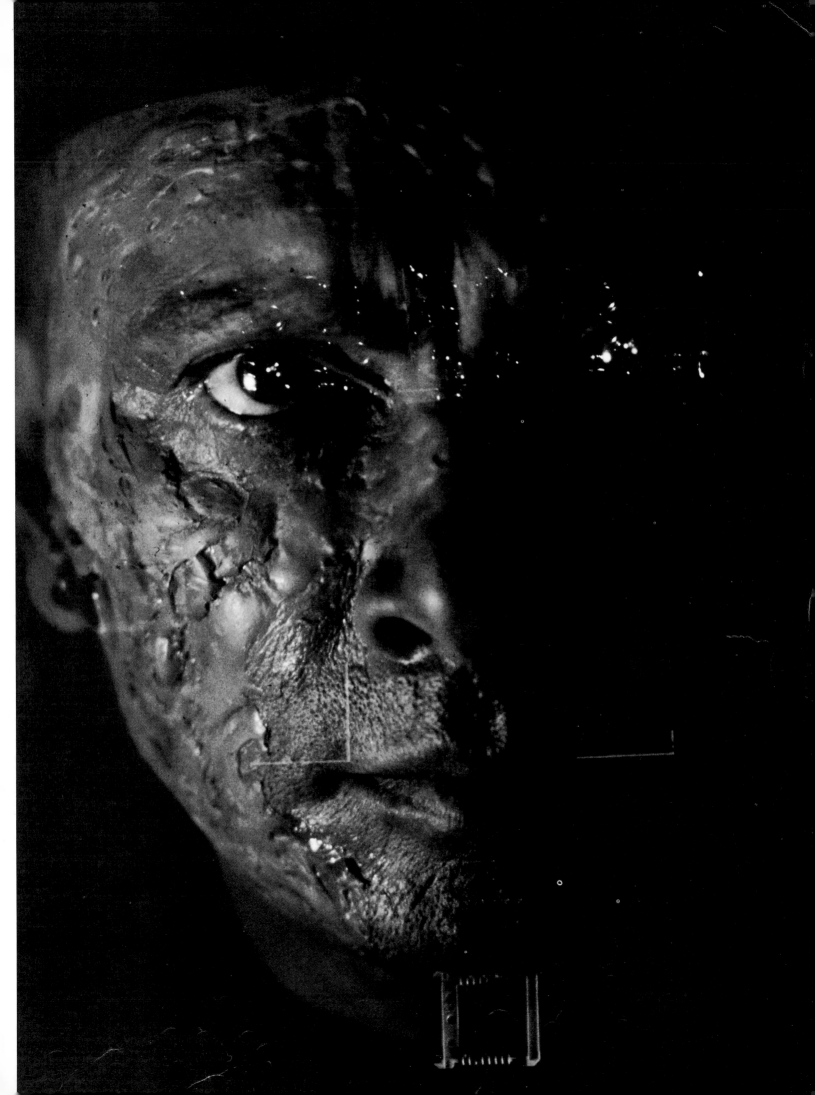

and dummies. One of the dummies appeared in a scene between Krige and Craig Wasson, when Krige transforms into a decaying corpse. "The dummy was made in a tremendous rush," recalls Smith. "We used the first one that came out of the mold. The foam latex was a little rigid. It was not perfect, but it was usable."

The Evil Dead (1982) aimed at equally stunning effects but on a very low budget. Tom Sullivan was the creative force behind the film's horrific illusions, but there was so little money for the makeup that he was forced to come up with his own formula for blood. This consisted of corn syrup, food coloring, a dash of instant coffee for thickening and a spoonful of starch for opacity. "The advantages of corn syrup", according to Sullivan, "are that you can put it in your mouth without too much discomfort, it stays shiny on clothes for weeks in case you have to reshoot scenes, and it doesn't collect the dust!"

The filming on **Evil Dead** was hard work for everyone involved, but one incident with one of Sullivan's

Nastassja Kinski bares her fangs as she undergoes a physical transformation in the film **Cat People** (1982). The actress's entire head is buried beneath several latex appliances, false teeth and contact lenses. Who said acting is an easy way to make a living?

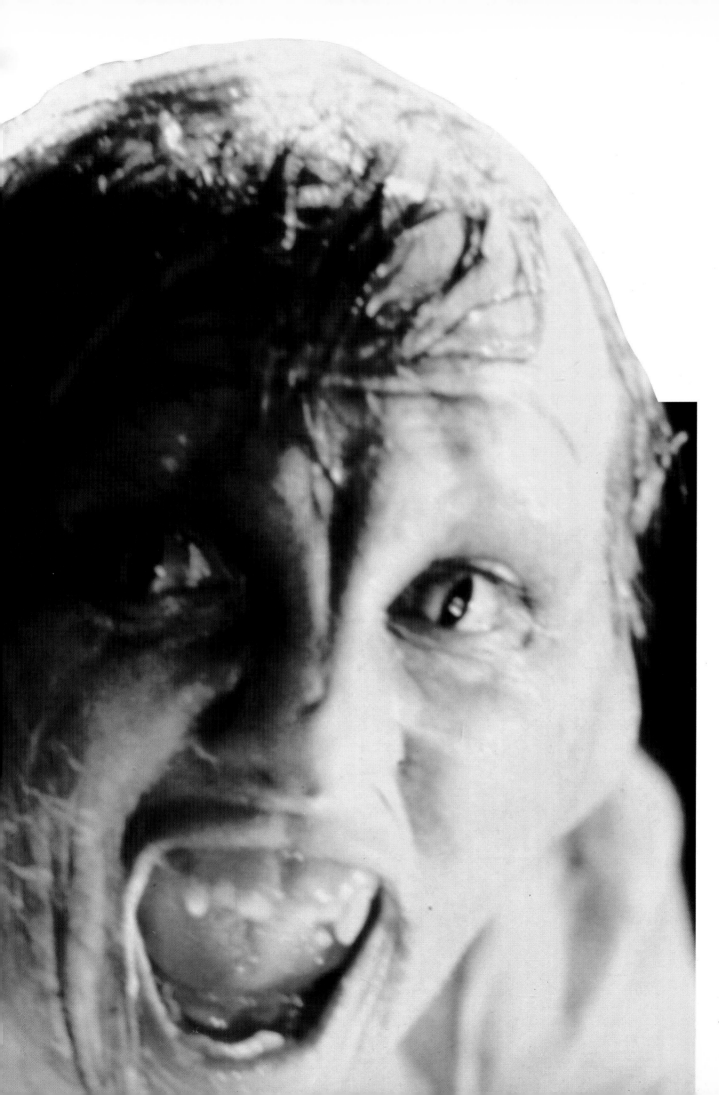

149

props momentarily relieved the tension. Sullivan had left the set, leaving behind a false arm stuffed with red meat. When he returned, the director's dog had dragged it out onto the street and was tucking into a good meal. A passing woman nearly had a heart attack when she saw Sullivan trying to wrestle the arm back off the dog.

Puppet power

Back in Hollywood, makeup wizard Rob Bottin had been contracted by director John Carpenter to create the makeup effects for **The Thing** (1982). The project was more an adaptation of the original short story that a remake of the 1951 movie **The Thing From Another World**, which meant that this time the Thing would have to be a bone fide shape-shifter, altering its shape in a variety of terrifying ways.

Nastassja Kinski undergoing the elaborate makeup for her role in **Cat People** (1982) under the supervision of Tom Burman. The first picture (*below*) shows Kinski as she appears during most of the film. The second (*above right*) shows makeup man Leonard Engleman attaching latex appliances to Kinski's face for an early stage of the transformation into a panther. The third picture (*below right*) has the full-head mask and body appliances in place for a later transformation.

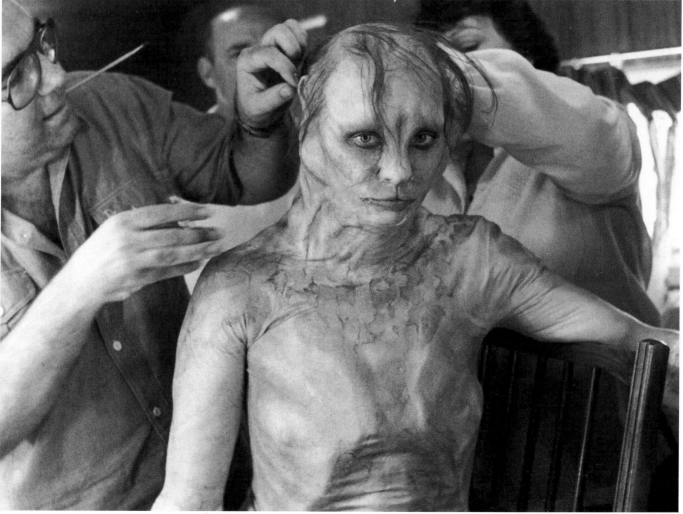

In this sequence of behind-the-scenes pictures from **The Company of Wolves**, the special makeup crew prepare a dummy of actor Stephen Rea. The first (*below*) shows makeup supervisor Chris Tucker and an assistant working on the dummy head. The second (*right*) shows an assistant fixing the dummy head to the dummy torso and attaching the control wires and cables which the crew use to put the dummy through its limited repertoire of movements.

Far right:
Technicians put the finishing touches to a dummy of actor Alfred Molina, about to be skewered in **Raiders of the Lost Ark** (1981). For details of its preparation, see pages 160-3.

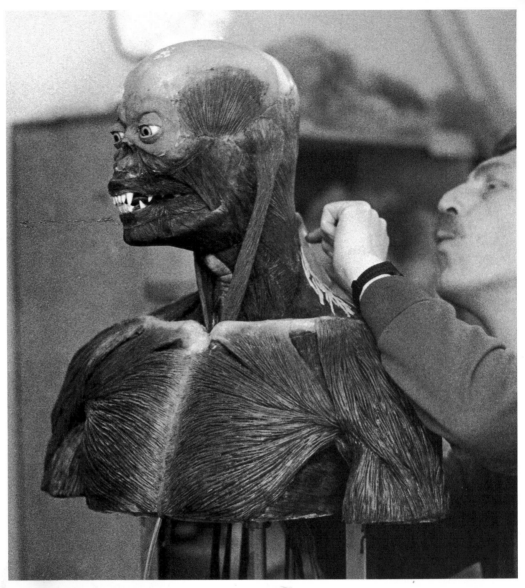

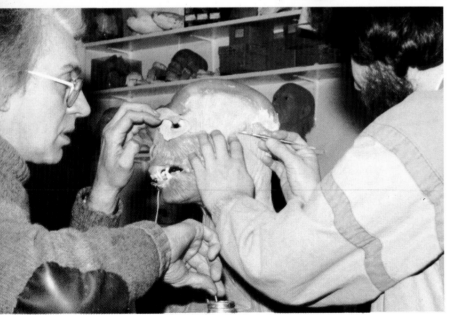

Bottin's main intention was to keep the audience off-guard, then surprise and entertain, always keeping them guessing. Of the many tricks used in **The Thing**, the most imaginative was probably the use of life-size puppets, particularly for the scenes where a man's tongue shoots out, wraps itself around his own head and then drags him across the room, and for that in which a chest bursts open to bite off someone's arms. The puppets so resembled real actors that audiences simply couldn't tell the difference.

Although **The Thing** was not a box-office hit, few could deny that it did contain some extraordinary effects. So far, the various incarnations of the Thing are unsurpassed for sheer weirdness. Bottin has remained fairly tight-lipped about just how he achieved the makeup effect for the film beyond saying that he relied on obvious techniques including hand puppets, marionettes, radio controls, wires, hydraulics and film reversing. Add to that a list of extra ingredients like bubble gum, strawberry jam, mayonnaise, cream corn and that same food thickener that was the basic constituent of **The Blob** (1958).

However, Bottin did not handle one major effect, the sequence in which the husky dog sheds its skin

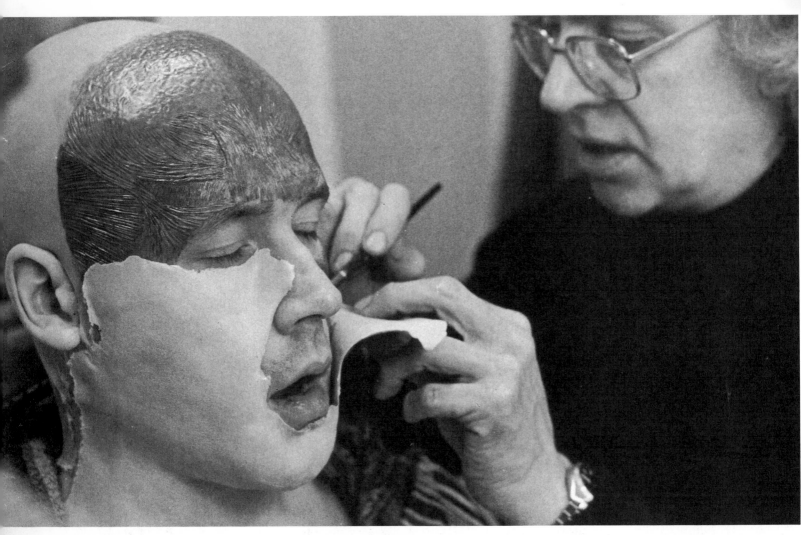

Preparing for a particularly grisly scene in **The Company of Wolves** (1984) in which Stephen Rea loses his skin. In the first picture (*above*), Christopher Tucker fits foam latex "skin" over the actor's already made-up face. The second (*right*) shows the latex skin almost completed. The third (*far right*) shows the effect when Rea rips away the fake skin.

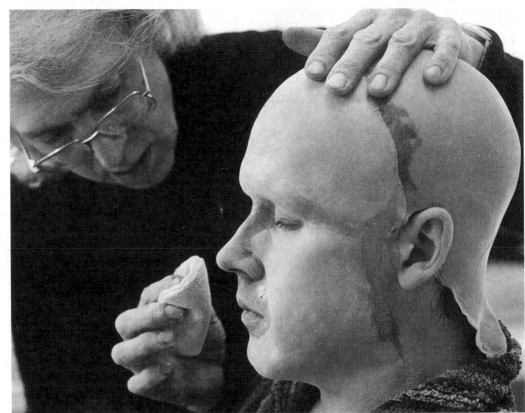

and turns inside out. "I'd already done **The Howling**," said Bottin, "and I did not want to *see* another dog. I didn't care if it was orange. I didn't care if it was riding a skateboard!" So Bottin handed the assignment over to Stanley Winston, the makeup artist on **Dead and Buried** (1981) and **Parasite** (1982). Winston had two main problems, inventing a creature that was both a dog and not a dog, and which also blended exactly with Bottin's other effects.

Far and away the most amazing effect in **The Thing** was the death of Norris, one of the men at the Antarctic station where the action takes place. Norris is apparently stricken with a heart attack and Dr Copper rushes to revive him with a cardiac defibrillator. Norris' chest splits open to reveal a huge set of jaws which bite Copper's hands off. Bedlam ensues. As the men turn the flame thrower on Norris his head falls off the edge of the table to the floor, apparently severing itself from the body. Once on the floor, the head sprouts a set of legs and scampers towards the open door like a huge spider. In that instant, the average audience doesn't know whether to laugh or

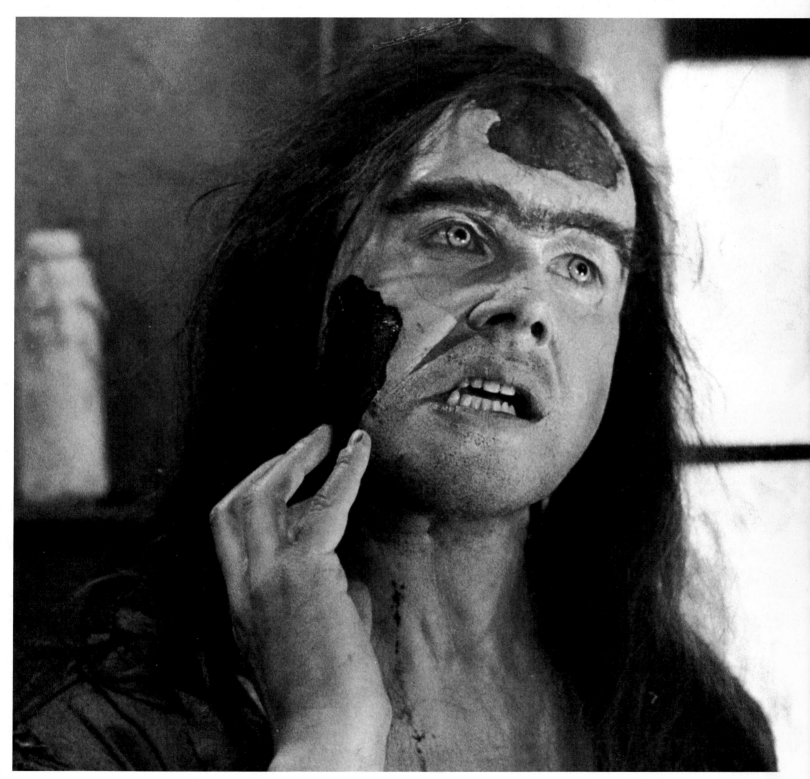

British makeup man Christopher Tucker works on part of the transformation sequence from **The Company of Wolves** (1984). A girl dries the latex "skin" of the dummy head with a hair dryer (*far left*). Then the dummy head – all its details now in place – has the final touches of color added (*this page*). In the final picture (*overleaf*) you can see why a dummy head was needed as a wolf's snout forces its way out of the apparently human mouth, accompanied by suitable, bone-crunching sound effects!

scream. The effects were achieved using the following techniques: Norris' body was a fiberglass dummy; Copper was doubled by a stand-in who had false hands which could be readily bitten off by the massive teeth in Norris' chest; Norris' head was pushed off by an off-screen technician holding a long rod. When the head sprouted spidery legs it is in fact sprouting thin-gauge, radio-controlled aluminum tubing; and the walking movement was achieved by attaching the legs to wheels which propelled the head across the floor, as the wheels turned faster, so the legs thrashed more violently. It was an arresting effect.

The **King Kong** (1977) and **Close Encounters of the Third Kind** (1977) makeup man was Carlo Rambaldi, drafted in by Steven Spielberg to design and execute the makeup for **E.T. The Extra-Terrestrial**. At the time, the filmmakers didn't reveal how E.T. was brought to life, but there wasn't really any secret to hide. For some shots E.T. was any one of several midgets in an E.T. mask. For others, the cute spaceman was one of Rambaldi's mechanical models, using the techniques developed by Rambaldi for his other creations.

These pages and overleaf: A "how to" sequence from Steven Spielberg's **Raiders of the Lost Ark** (1981). Chris Walas and his team are creating a life-sized replica of actor Alfred Molina which is about to be impaled on one of the many traps seen during the opening sequence of the film. In order to ensure the dummy exactly resembles the actor, a life-cast is taken of his head, an especially unpleasant experience for the "victim".

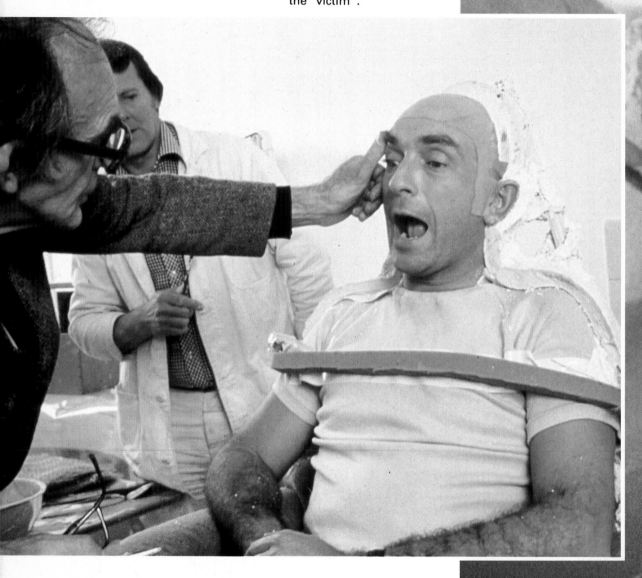

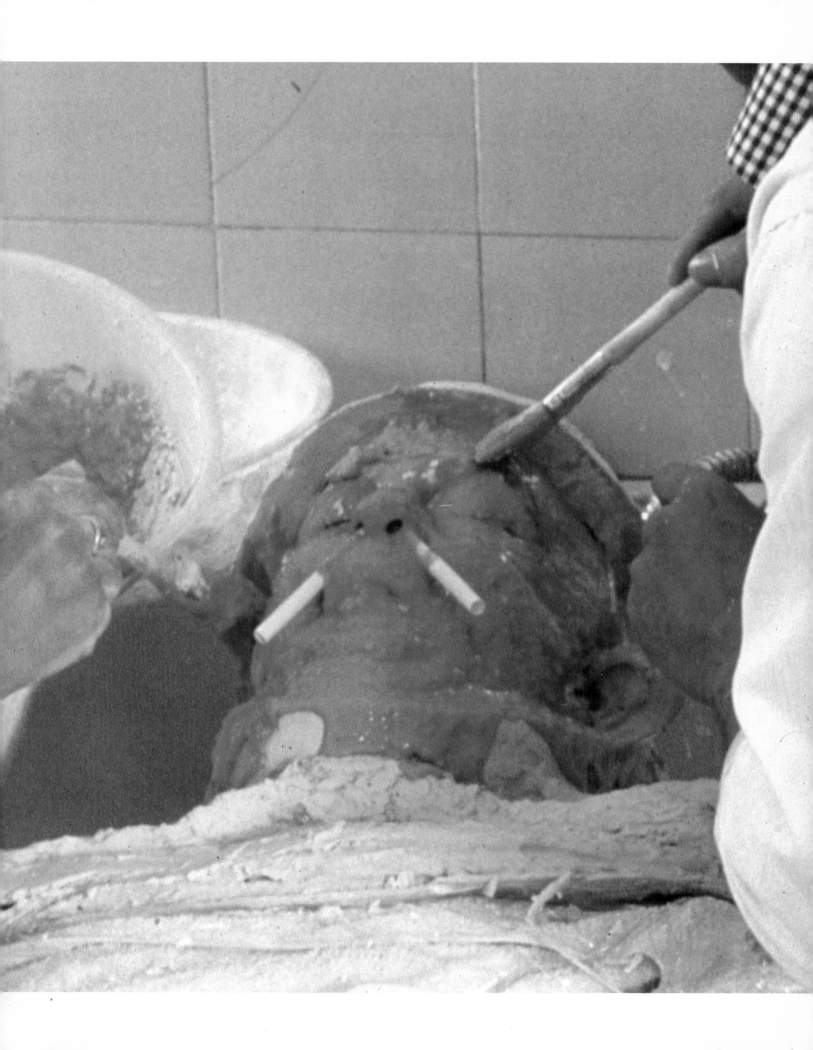

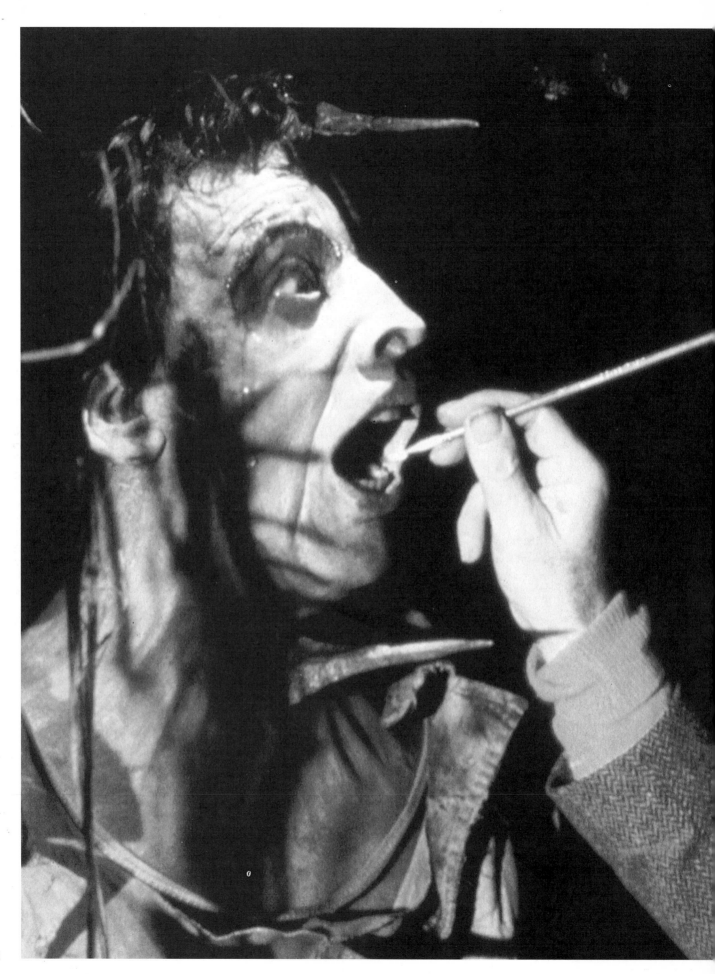

The other big makeup movie of 1982 was Paul Schrader's remake of the classic **Cat People**. The central makeup scene in the film occurs when star Nastassja Kinski transforms into a panther, using techniques similar to those used by Bottin and Baker on **The Howling** and **An American Werewolf** respectively. Tom Burman, the makeup artist responsible for the transformation, revealed how they managed the film's main effects. When Kinski changes, with her skin splitting and falling away to reveal a snarling panther's head, the cameras close in on an artificial expanding head made up of expandable pneumatics. In order to get the eyes to retract, they set artificial ones at the ends of two long tubes.

Ghostbusters

Though primarily a horror movie relying on special effects, **Poltergeist** did have one rather attention-grabbing makeup scene. This is where one of the ghost-busters has a nasty experience with a lump of steak in the kitchen and rushes, a little queasy, to a nearby handbasin to splash some water on his face. Audiences are amazed when the unfortunate character looks at himself in the mirror above the sink to see his fingers wiping the skin from his face. Suddenly it disintegrates, the fingers dislodging great chunks of flesh.

Chief makeup man Craig Reardon made a duplicate of the actor's head, set with an agonized expression and then covered with a gelatinous substance. "Goo" was pumped in to look like blood. When it came to filming, producer Steven Spielberg sat on a box beneath the head and reached up to claw the face right down to the bone. The film features his hands and not those of the actor. By the end of the day's shooting he was covered in blood and gore but apparently loved it! The only disappointing aspect was that the makeup department didn't have sufficient time to perfect the false head – though no one noticed.

Transforming actors into horrific monsters doesn't seem so difficult when you compare this with creating an aging process that uses dummy heads that simulate aging past death and well into corpsedom. That is what veteran makeup man Bob Schiffer was required to produce for the 1983 Disney production of **Something Wicked This Way Comes**. In the climax of the film, Mr. Dark, the villain played by Jonathan Pryce, withers away in a time trap of his own making. This was the first time anyone had attempted such an effect. The main problem was in managing an easy transition from the human to the mechanical head. It had to be a perfect match – there was no room for error. The puppets were precise anatomical replicas, right down to their mouth and eye movements.

The Company of Wolves (1984) must be the last word on men changing into wolves. Christopher Tucker, who turned John Hurt into the Elephant Man, was hired to turn an actor into a wolf, but from the inside. In one stunning sequence, a man opens his mouth to allow a wolf's muzzle to protrude. The wolf's snout keeps on coming, stretching the actor's mouth horribly, until the wolf's head breaks into full view. **The Elephant Man** had been a difficult film to

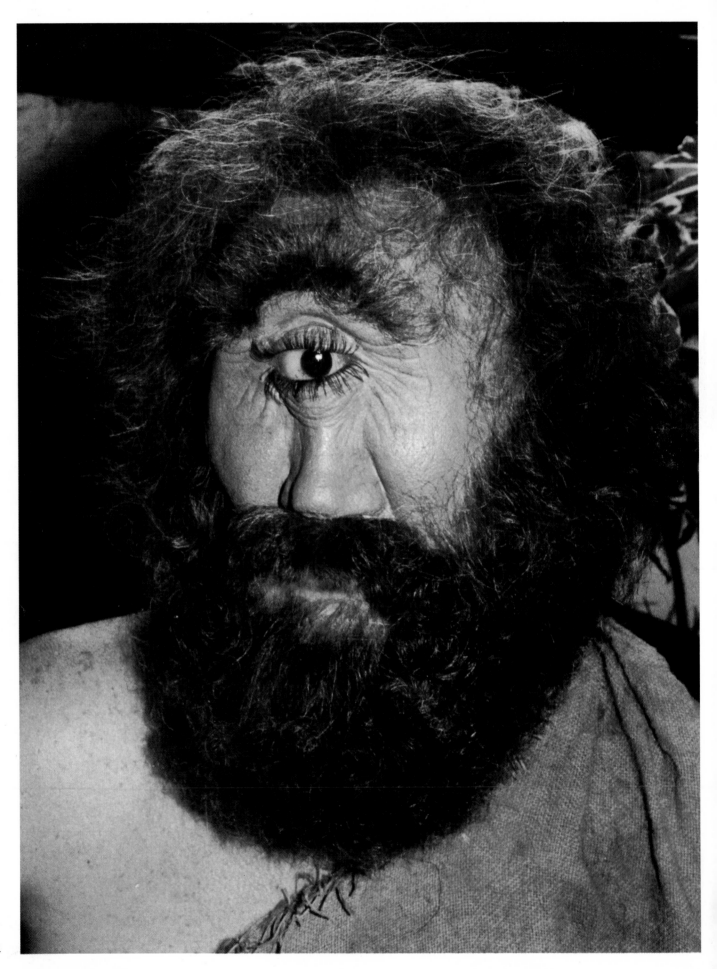

make, but this one involved an entirely different set of problems. So many and so intricate were they, that it was decided to film at dress rehearsals in case anything went wrong. The original idea had been to turn the whole of the hunter's face inside out revealing a wolf, but it was impossible to realize this effect on schedule. Instead, they settled on a dummy with radio controlled eyes.

Conclusion

The great strength of the cinema is that now, more than ever before, it has the ability to depict almost every aspect of the writer's and director's imagination. Nothing need be left to *our* imagination. Consequently, the modern screen in particular has been blessed, as we have seen, with extraordinary images that constantly challenge our expectations and delight. It seems that the only restrictions, just as they were back at the turn of the century, are those of strict production budgets and schedules.

Left:
In the country of the blind, the one-eyed man is king. . . . British makeup wizard Christopher Tucker (*below*) rises to yet another challenge by creating the mythical Cyclops in human form. (*Pictures courtesy of Christopher Tucker*)

Overleaf:
A classic example from **The Fury** (1978) of Dick Smith's "mole" in action. The effect is achieved using a couple of rubber bladders (inflated by off-camera technicians) under a foam latex appliance. When the set-up is operated it looks as though something is pulsating under Andrew Stevens' skin.

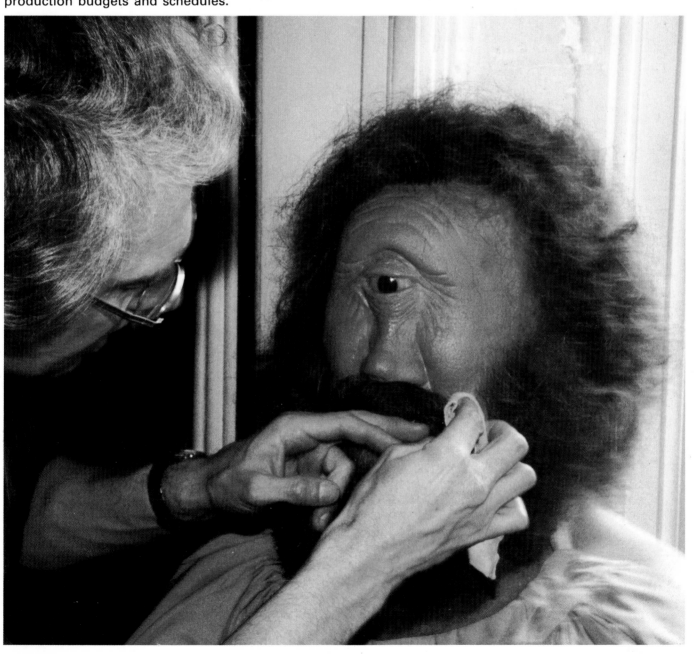

Blinding
Broken
4/21/93